EFF ANGER MANAGEMENT FOR TEENS

HANDLE FRUSTRATION, STOP THE RAGE, AND BUILD A HAPPIER
LIFE - NAVIGATE THE STORMS OF ADOLESCENCE WITH
MINDFULNESS, EMPATHY, AND STRENGTH

Emma Davis

Impact
— PUBLISHING —

TABLE OF CONTENTS

This page has been intentionally left blank

INTRODUCTION

If you are patient in one moment of anger, you will escape a hundred days of sorrow.

– Chinese Proverb

HAVE YOU EVER felt a storm brewing inside you, so powerful that it threatened to break free and wreak havoc? If you're a teenager or someone who cares deeply about one, you know this storm all too well. It's the storm of anger—a fierce, often misunderstood emotion that can feel as much a part of you as your own heartbeat. But what if I told you that within this storm lies not just the potential for destruction, but also the power for incredible change? This is not just a guide; it's a voyage into the heart of your tempest, where we'll learn to harness this power together, transforming it into a force for self-control, better relationships, and emotional well-being.

In this journey, we're not just looking to 'manage' anger in the traditional sense—where feelings are suppressed, and emotions are tucked away. Instead, we're aiming to understand its roots, communicate its messages effectively, and channel its energy constructively. This approach isn't about denying what you feel; it's about embracing your emotions as valuable signals, guiding you towards understanding yourself and how you interact with the world around you.

In writing this book, I draw upon my extensive experience and expertise as a clinical social worker and therapist. Through my work with adolescents facing various practical and emotional challenges, I have witnessed firsthand what anger can do to the growing impressionable minds of teens. Neither am I new to kids and their tantrums, as a mother of nine children, I understand the ups and downs of adolescence. My experience has taught me that a great number of adolescents are at a crossroads, on the verge of undergoing a transition, and searching for a way to deal with the maze of their own emotions. The emotion of anger, which is a continuous companion for many people, has the potential to either stoke the flames of destruction or, if appropriate, shed light on the path to personal development and empowerment. This book is a lighthouse for individuals who are lost in the darkness, providing a way for them to find their way back to themselves and the powerful potential that lies inside them.

Anger can be a quite deadly beast — hard to manage on your own. As a result of the challenges that adolescents face, such as social pressure, scholastic stress, the search for identity, and the battle for autonomy, this beast seems to grow even more fearsome by the time they reach their teenage years. Anger whispers falsehoods of isolation, that you are alone in your rage, that no one understands, and that there is no way to contain the wildfire burning inside you.

However, the truth contains freedom in multitudes. It liberates you. When it is listened to with intention, anger is not a beast but rather a signal, a message that may lead to deep self-awareness and real transformation. Imagine a teenager, Alex, who feels a surge of anger every time they're interrupted while talking. On the surface, this anger might seem like a simple reaction to frustration. However, by listening to this anger with intention, Alex begins to understand it's not just about being interrupted; it's a deep-seated feeling of being unheard and undervalued that's been lingering for years.

This realization came to Alex during a family dinner, a common scenario where interruptions were frequent. Instead of lashing out as usual, Alex decided to reflect on why this specific action sparked such intense anger. Through journaling about the experience and discussing it in a calm moment with a family member, Alex discovered that this anger was actually a signal pointing towards a need for respect and to be valued within their family dynamic.

Guided by this new understanding, Alex initiated a conversation with their family about communication styles and the importance of being heard. This not only improved their family interactions but also empowered Alex to express their feelings and needs more clearly in other relationships, leading to a positive transformation in Alex'emotional world.

The purpose of this book is to dispel the myths that surround anger, to dispel the fear and misunderstanding that often accompany it, and to unveil the power and knowledge that rage can give. My dedication to empowering young people extends beyond writing—I run a therapy practice and financial education agency tailored to teenagers, and I offer online courses covering interpersonal skills, gratitude, and happiness. With this breadth of experience and knowledge, I find myself uniquely positioned to guide readers through the transformative journey of understanding and managing their anger effectively. It's almost an urge and a sense of responensibility that has motivated this endeavor.

In this book, you will engage in a journey of discovery and investigation as you make your way through these pages. You will investigate the neuroscience that underlies anger, gaining an understanding of how the brain of a teenager operates in a variety of distinct ways that impact emotional reactions. You will acquire the ability to differentiate between experiencing anger and acting on that anger, and you will come to see that the space that exists between the two is where your sphere of influence is located.

This path is not simply about learning how to control your anger; rather, it is about gaining a deeper awareness of who you are. It is important to recognize your triggers, but it is equally important to comprehend the reasons for their existence. The key is to see the patterns that emerge in your responses and to acquire the skills necessary to rewrite those scripts. Through this experience, you will learn how to communicate your needs and feelings in a manner that is constructive rather than destructive — one that encourages connection rather than causing distance.

Once you have this knowledge, you will be presented with a toolset of tactics that are not only meant to help you cope, but also to help you thrive more effectively. A variety of tools are available to you, including methods for mindfulness that assist you in maintaining your equilibrium in the midst of the storm, communication skills that enable you to open

EFFECTIVE ANGER MANAGEMENT FOR TEEN

doors rather than shut them, and creative outlets that enable you to productively channel your energy.

For the purpose of producing a thorough guide that moves from comprehension to action, each chapter is organized in such a way that it builds upon the previous one. You will acquire the knowledge and skills necessary to swiftly calm down through the use of practical exercises, techniques for constructive confrontation, and tactics for reflecting on your anger at the present time. This book does not provide a solution that is universally applicable; rather, it provides a customization strategy that takes into account your uniqueness.

Entailed in this book are the experiences of young people who, like you, have confronted their feelings of anger and emerged from the experience more resilient than before. This is not only a collection of success tales; rather, it is a genuine description of the fight, the failures, and the little triumphs that ultimately result in significant improvements. By reading these experiences, you will realize that you are not the only one experiencing these emotions or difficulties. There is a community of people around you who have been on this journey before you, who have confronted the beast and discovered how to coexist with it in a harmonious manner. This book is built on that hope.

Why Should You Read This Book?

At this point, you may be wondering why I have decided to be your guide along this adventure. My journey in the field of psychology and my work with adolescents have spanned several key roles, each offering unique insights and challenges that have enriched my understanding of emotional and behavioral dynamics in youth.

In this capacity, I've conducted one-on-one therapy sessions with teenagers, addressing issues ranging from mild anxiety and stress to more complex conditions like depression and anger management. These intimate settings have allowed for deep dives into the individual experiences of anger, its triggers, and its effects on personal and social functioning.

Working within educational institutions, I've had the privilege of guiding young people through the everyday challenges of adolescence. This role has involved both proactive educational initiatives to teach students about emotional regulation and reactive interventions to mediate conflicts and provide support in crisis situations.

My journey into the heart of anger and back isn't just a professional pursuit; it's a personal expedition marked by both challenge and discovery. My foundation in this field is built upon a robust academic background in psychology, where I delved into the complexities of human emotions and behavior, earning degrees that not only provided me with a deep understanding of theoretical concepts but also equipped me with the tools to apply these insights in practical settings.

Beyond the classrooms and textbooks, my professional path has led me to work closely with adolescents, guiding them through their most turbulent years. This work has spanned various settings—from private practice and school counseling to community mental health programs. Each experience has enriched my perspective, allowing me to witness firsthand the transformative power of addressing anger constructively.

However, the most compelling aspect of my expertise comes from navigating my own storms of anger. Like many, I've felt the fierce grip of unspoken frustrations and the isolation that can accompany misunderstood emotions. My personal journey through understanding my anger—learning to listen to its messages, and harnessing its energy for positive change—has been both challenging and enlightening. This path has not only deepened my empathy and connection with those I help but has also solidified my belief in the potential for personal growth and transformation through the intentional exploration of our emotions.

Equipped with this blend of professional expertise and personal experience, I stand before you not just as a guide, but as a fellow traveler. This book is an invitation to walk together on a journey of understanding, transforming the way we view and interact with our anger. It's about turning what often feels like an enemy into one of our most insightful allies, leading us toward greater self-awareness, improved relationships, and emotional well-being.

I have experience both the pain of words that were left unsaid, and the sorrow of words that cannot be taken back. My experience has shown me that allowing anger to fester uncontrolled may result in the loss of opportunities, relationships, and even one's own sense of self-respect.

However, what is more significant is that I have realized the transforming potential of comprehending and controlling that power of fury. I am not making these teachings available to you from a position of superiority; rather, I am doing it from a point of shared experience and empathy. The reason I am here to assist you is not because I have never failed; rather, it is because I have failed in the past and yet I have managed to overcome it.

I want to encourage you to take a brave step forward despite the fact that we are standing together on the precipice of this trip. This book is more than simply a guidebook; it is a call to action—a call to face and accept your feelings, to improve your relationship with anger, and to find the unstoppable feeling of summer that is inside you.

If that's the case, let's get started. By working together, we will investigate the terrain of your feelings and discover the instruments and methods that you need in order to successfully traverse the complexity of rage. We will examine the misconceptions, confront the anxieties, and by the time you reach the conclusion, you will not only have a more profound under tending of your anger, but also a thorough strategy for using it as a driving force for personal development and transformation.

Together, let's take that first step into a journey that promises to transform not just how you cope with anger, but also how you perceive yourself and your role in the world.

CHAPTER 1

The Nature of Anger in Teenage Life

> *For every minute you remain angry, you give up sixty seconds of peace of mind.*
>
> – Ralph Waldo Emerson

A POWERFUL ENERGY THROUGHOUT adolescence is anger, which is often misunderstood and denigrated. Whether it's bubbling up1 during an argument, brewing beneath the surface, or driving one towards unforeseen obstacles or transformations, it may pop out at any moment. But deep down, rage is only a message that, when understood, may show us a lot about our limits, priorities, and wants. This chapter dispels popularly held beliefs about anger and its causes by studying the nature of this rage. Understanding the multifaceted nature of anger is just the beginning. It's what we choose to do with this understanding that truly reshapes our world. By intentionally engaging with our rage, not as an adversary but as a guide, we initiate a profound journey of self-discovery and growth. This isn't merely theoretical—it's a practical pathway to transformation. As we apply these insights, committing to a journey of intentional reflection and action, we begin to see tangible shifts in our lives and relationships.

Let's explore how this journey unfolds, leading us to two pivotal outcomes that redefine our interaction with anger.

Incident 1

Situation: A minor disagreement occurs between a parent and their adolescent child.

Reaction: The adolescent child reacts by yelling at the parent, losing control over their emotions in the heat of the moment.

Incident 2

Situation: A similar minor disagreement occurs, involving another adolescent.

Reaction: This adolescent chooses to retreat silently into their room, avoiding direct confrontation but still seething with rage internally.

Despite the stark differences in these reactions—one external and explosive, the other internal and suppressed—both are driven by the same underlying emotion: rage. The variance in responses can be attributed to a complex interplay of factors, including the unique workings of the adolescent brain, which is still developing its ability to regulate emotions; individual experiences, which shape how one learns to express or suppress emotions; and cultural expectations, which dictate the socially acceptable ways to display anger. These examples illustrate that while rage can manifest in vastly different behaviors, understanding its root and influences is crucial in addressing the emotional needs underlying these reactions.

In this chapter, we will dispel some of the most common misconceptions about anger and examine its dual nature as a problem and a chance for personal development. We will also examine the special connection between anger and the adolescent brain. Understanding and empathy are vital to managing the ups and downs of adolescent rage, which this chapter seeks to illuminate via anecdotes, data, and current research.

The Nature of Anger in Teens

Adolescence is a period marked by profound transformations that extend beyond the visible physical growth. It's a time of intense hormonal surges and significant neurological development, which can create a whirlwind of emotions and reactions that both teens and their guardians often find perplexing. The exploration of anger, particularly in the context of these adolescent changes, is crucial for understanding why emotions can seem so amplified during these years.

As Charles Spielberger, PhD, a psychologist with a career dedicated to studying anger, notes, anger spans a broad spectrum from mild annoyance to intense fury and hatred. This isn't merely an emotional shift; it's accompanied by tangible hormonal and physiological changes. For instance, when anger stirs, there's an observable increase in adrenaline and noradrenaline levels. This hormonal response triggers a cascade of physical reactions, such as an accelerated heart rate and elevated blood pressure, preparing the body for a perceived threat or challenge. These reactions are part of the body's fight-or-flight response, a survival mechanism that, while vital, can lead to heightened states of aggression or withdrawal in situations where such intense reactions are not warranted.

> Understanding the physiological changes behind adolescent anger is pivotal for navigating these turbulent emotions with empathy and effectiveness.

Understanding these physiological changes is pivotal, especially in adolescents whose hormonal landscapes are already in flux. This period of rapid and sometimes confusing change can make the experiences of anger particularly intense, leaving teens feeling overwhelmed or, conversely, disconnected from their emotions. By situating our exploration of anger within the broader context of adolescent development, we aim to shed light on how these biological shifts play a critical role in the way anger is experienced and expressed. Recognizing the underlying biological processes can empower both teens and those around them to navigate these turbulent waters with greater empathy and effectiveness, ultimately leading to healthier ways of managing and expressing anger.

Both internal and environmental factors might contribute to the development of anger. Anger might be directed at a particular individual (like a boss or colleague), a particular situation (like a traffic congestion or a cancelled trip), or it can be a result of dwelling on or worrying about issues in your personal life. The recollection of upsetting or painful experiences may often set off intense emotions of anger.

The wrath of teenagers is well-known, often leaving parents navigating the challenging waters of mood swings, door-slamming, and defiance. Far from being a mere cliché, these behaviors can present real and pressing challenges in the dynamics of family life.

Parents may feel like they're always on high alert due to their children's explosive tempers, erratic mood swings, and constant bickering over seemingly little matters such as who gets to put the dishes away or who goes to school.

This behavior is not always related to your actions or inactions since teenagers going through puberty have naturally heightened emotions. Anger outbursts from your adolescent are inevitable, regardless of how excellent a parent you are.

But you likely want to do something to help, particularly if their rage causes them to damage themselves, be violent, or cause problems with friends or family.

Did You Know?

While there's no singular "anger hormone," adrenaline and noradrenaline released by the adrenal glands under stress trigger the fight-or-flight response, increasing heart rate and energy. Additionally, rising cortisol levels heighten arousal and vigilance during anger episodes.

Hormonal Havoc

In the whirlwind of adolescent development, hormones emerge as pivotal players, wielding considerable influence over both physical maturation and emotional volatility. Among these, three primary hormones—testosterone, estrogen, and cortisol—play crucial roles in modulating emotions like anger.

Testosterone, often associated with aggressive behavior, sees a significant surge during puberty, especially in boys. This increase can intensify feelings of aggression and competitiveness, contributing to the expression of anger. Research has shown that heightened levels of testosterone are correlated with increased irritability and impulsiveness, factors that can amplify angry outbursts.

Estrogen, while commonly linked to female reproductive health, also affects mood and emotion regulation in both sexes. Fluctuations in estrogen levels can lead to mood swings and increased sensitivity to stress, thereby influencing how anger is experienced and expressed. Studies have indicated that estrogen can enhance the stress response, potentially leading to more frequent or intense episodes of anger.

Cortisol, known as the stress hormone, plays a direct role in the body's fight-or-flight response. Elevated cortisol levels, especially in stressful environments, can heighten the sense of agitation and readiness to react defensively, including with anger. Persistent high levels of cortisol can impair the prefrontal cortex's ability to regulate emotions, making it harder to control angry feelings.

The interplay of these hormones during adolescence does more than just "amp up" feelings; it fundamentally alters the brain's chemistry and structure, particularly in areas responsible for emotion regulation and decision-making. For instance, the prefrontal cortex, which is crucial for impulse control and empathy, is still maturing in teenagers. This developmental stage, combined with hormonal fluctuations, can make adolescents more prone to experiencing and expressing anger in ways that seem disproportionate to the triggering event.

Case Study: Ethan's Journey Through Hormonal Changes and Anger Management

Ethan, a 15-year-old high school sophomore, has been increasingly noted by his parents and teachers for his short temper and aggressive reactions to relatively minor annoyances. Previously known for his calm demeanor, Ethan's sudden change in behavior raised concerns, prompting a referral to a school psychologist for assessment.

Behavioral Changes: Ethan displayed a marked increase in irritability, with several instances of verbal outbursts directed at teachers and peers. Additionally, Ethan's participation in sports led to observations of heightened competitiveness, sometimes culminating in aggressive confrontations with teammates.

Academic Performance: A decline in Ethan's academic performance was noted, particularly in situations requiring sustained attention and patience, which seemed to exacerbate his frustration.

Assessment

Hormonal Evaluation: Blood tests revealed elevated testosterone levels, common in adolescent males but notably high in Ethan's case. Additionally, cortisol levels indicated a heightened stress response, likely contributing to his quick temper and aggression.

Psychological Evaluation: The assessment underscored Ethan's difficulty in managing stress and navigating the emotional turmoil associated with his developmental stage. It also revealed Ethan's lack of effective coping mechanisms for his anger.

Intervention

Cognitive-Behavioral Therapy (CBT): Ethan was introduced to CBT to help him recognize the triggers of his anger, understand the connection between his thoughts, emotions, and reactions, and develop healthier coping strategies.

Stress Management Techniques: Techniques such as deep breathing exercises, mindfulness, and physical activity were recommended to help Ethan manage his stress levels and reduce his cortisol levels.

Family Counseling: Sessions were conducted to educate Ethan's family on the physiological and psychological aspects of adolescence, equipping them with strategies to support Ethan through this transitional period.

Outcome: Over the course of several months, Ethan showed significant improvements in his ability to manage anger and stress. He became more adept at identifying the early signs of frustration and employing coping strategies before reaching a boiling point. His relationships with peers and family improved, as did his academic performance, illustrating the effectiveness of addressing the underlying hormonal influences and equipping Ethan with practical skills for emotional regulation.

> Understanding the complex relationship between changing hormone levels, growing brains, and the quest for self-discovery is crucial for navigating the whirlwind of adolescent fury with empathy and effectiveness.

Brain in the Process of Growth

In adolescence, the prefrontal cortex—a region responsible for controlling impulses, making decisions, and understanding the consequences of one's actions—is still in the process of being built.

This developmental lag can leave teenagers navigating a tumultuous landscape of emotions without the full suite of cognitive tools necessary for nuanced responses. Because of this gap in development, people's fury might flare up unexpectedly and disproportionately, akin to wielding a sledgehammer when a scalpel would be more appropriate. This metaphor illustrates not just the intensity but also the lack of precision with which adolescents might respond to situations that require a more measured approach, underscoring the challenges they face in managing their emotions effectively.

Identity Crisis and Personal Freedom

Identity development and the pursuit of autonomy are two further hallmarks of adolescence. As they discover who they are and push the limits of accepted behavior, teenagers on this path often find themselves in conflict with one another. Anger may be a powerful expression of independence or discontent with injustices that one perceives. Getting through this stage is important, but it may be confusing for the people helping the teens and for the teens themselves as they go through these feelings.

Simultaneously, the pursuit of autonomy—a desire to become self-governing and independent—often puts teenagers at odds with existing societal norms and family expectations, leading to inevitable conflicts. Such conflicts are not merely personal struggles but are situated within a broader sociocultural and structural framework that both constrains and facilitates identity exploration. Teenagers, in their quest for autonomy, might challenge accepted behaviors and norms, using anger as a powerful tool to assert their emerging identities and express discontent with perceived injustices.

The sociological perspective emphasizes that these conflicts and the accompanying emotional turmoil are not just natural but necessary for healthy development. However, navigating through this stage can be particularly challenging for both the adolescents, who are in the throes of discovering who they are, and for those supporting them. The complexities of identity formation are compounded by the diverse influences of peer groups, media, and broader societal expectations, which can all serve as sources of conflict and, consequently, emotional expressions such as anger.

Understanding the sociological underpinnings of identity development and autonomy can provide valuable insights for parents, educators, and counselors. Recognizing that these expressions of anger and conflict are part of a larger process of becoming can facilitate more empathetic and supportive approaches to guiding adolescents through this critical period of their lives. It underscores the importance of creating spaces where teenagers can safely explore and express their evolving identities while learning to navigate the societal structures that shape their experiences.

The Expression Spectrum

There is a wide range of angry expressions among teens. A lot of people let their frustrations out in the form of violent or verbal attacks, but other people bottle it up and end up being very negative to themselves. Dissimilarities in how rage is "appropriately" conveyed may arise from a variety of sources, including individual variances, coping mechanisms, and cultural gender norms. This has the potential to stifle constructive expression of emotions while reinforcing damaging preconceptions.

Consider Aliya and Reema, two teenagers attending the same high school but coming from different cultural backgrounds. Aliya, who is raised in a family that values stoicism and control over emotional expression, has been taught that displaying anger is inappropriate and unbecoming, especially for women. As a result, she tends to suppress her feelings of frustration, leading her to internalize her anger. This often manifests as silent withdrawal or passive-aggressive behavior, since she's learned that overt expressions of anger would conflict with her cultural and gender expectations. Her preferred coping mechanism is writing in a journal, allowing her a private outlet to process her emotions without breaking the norms she's been taught to uphold.

Reema, on the other hand, comes from a background that encourages open emotional expression, viewing it as a healthy and necessary aspect of personal development. However, she finds herself dealing with societal gender norms that unfairly label women as overly emotional if they express anger too openly. Struggling to balance her family's encouragement for expression with the broader societal stigma, Reema often opts for assertive communication as a way to express her anger constructively. She engages in debates and discussions, both in person and on social media, as a means to channel her frustration into advocacy and change, aiming to confront and shift the damaging stereotypes that stigmatize women's anger.

These contrasting experiences of Aliya and Reema highlight the complex interplay between individual coping mechanisms and the cultural and gender norms dictating the "appropriate" ways to express anger. Their stories highlight how societal expectations can not only stifle the constructive expression of emotions but also reinforce harmful stereotypes, making it crucial to recognize and validate diverse emotional expressions across different cultural and gender backgrounds.

Empathy and Understanding

A little neurobiology, along with tolerance and empathy, is required to recognize the complex dynamics of adolescent fury. Understanding the source of the emotional storm is just as important as weathering it. We can better assist teenagers if we understand the complex relationship between their changing hormone levels, their growing brains, and their quest for self-discovery. Even though it's a rough patch, this stage is full with learning and development opportunities. Adolescents, with the help of adults who understand and empathize with them, may learn to control their anger and use it for good, instead of making things worse.

The Teenage Brain and Anger

Has it ever occurred to you why being a teenager is like being in the middle of a storm? Things are going swimmingly one second, and then you're in the middle of a raging storm of emotions, most notably fury.

This emotional maelstrom is at its core not just due to hormones going rampant, but also to an intriguing and complicated dance taking place in the adolescent brain.

An Evolving Mind

In the mind of adolescent, there is a work of art in progress, a landscape being built. Consider a home improvement project that involves updating the plumbing and electrical while the occupants continue to reside in the property. Your brain throughout adolescence looks like that. The processing and expression of emotions, such as rage, are significantly influenced by this stage of brain development, which is one of the most important following infancy.

The Amygdala, the Center of Emotions

The almond-shaped collection of neurons known as the amygdala is the emotional epicenter of this turmoil. It acts as an early warning system in the brain, always monitoring for threats to one's emotional well-being and ability to survive. The amygdala goes into overdrive, heightened sensitivity, and reactiveness throughout adolescence. Because of this

> Navigating teenage fury requires understanding the intricate dance between the overactive amygdala and the still-developing prefrontal cortex in the adolescent brain.

increased sensitivity, feelings may be more powerful, more real, and even overpowering at times. The amygdala is responsible for setting off the alert when anger sets in, and it does so more forcefully and urgently than it does in later life.

The Frontal Lobe: A Reasoning Voice

The area of the brain in charge of thinking, planning, and self-control is the prefrontal cortex, which you will now meet. It makes judgments and considers the repercussions like the head of the brain. The problem? This chief executive officer is still in his formative years. When a person reaches their mid-20s, they have fully developed the prefrontal cortex, one of the brain's later sections.

If the amygdala were an overprotective security system and the prefrontal cortex was an inefficient monitoring center, it would be like having a developmental gap between the two. What is the outcome? Anger and other emotional reactions may be rapid, strong, and excessive at times.

Making Connections: Brain Routes

The brain's wiring undergoes substantial modifications during adolescence. We are strengthening and pruning neural pathways, which are the paths by which the brain communicates with itself. Pathways that are utilized regularly are strengthened and those that aren't, get trimmed away; this process is based on the "use it or lose it" concept. The way teenagers see and respond to their environment and their emotions is impacted by this remodeling. That's why the habits we develop during this time, whether they're good ways to cope or not, may affect us for a long time.

The Importance of Background and Situation

Not only does biology have a hand in writing this screenplay, but experience and environment are also major players. Adolescents' environments, the actions they see, and the criticism they get, all play a role in how they learn to control their anger. Conflicts may be transformed into learning opportunities when they are taught healthy methods to manage anger in a caring and understanding atmosphere.

Jordan, a 13-year-old, had a major tantrum over being asked to turn off the video game and start homework. The frustration wasn't just about stopping a preferred activity; it was also about feeling controlled and not having a say in personal time management. This moment of anger was intense, marked by yelling and a refusal to comply with the request, reflecting a deeper struggle with autonomy and the desire for independence.

Jordan's parent, recognizing the tantrum as more than just a reaction to the immediate request, decided to approach the situation with empathy rather than punishment. Once Jordan had cooled down slightly, the parent sat down with him to discuss not just the importance of schoolwork but also to listen to Jordan's feelings about autonomy and control over personal time. They worked together to establish a new schedule that allowed for gaming time and homework, based on mutual respect and understanding. This approach showed Jordan that his feelings were valid and that conflicts could be resolved through communication.

This incident had a profound effect on Jordan's relationship with anger. Instead of viewing anger as an enemy or a trigger for punishment, Jordan learned to see it as a signal for deeper needs or conflicts that required attention. Over time, Jordan became more adept at identifying the reasons behind feelings of anger and more willing to engage in open dialogue to address them. This transformation also improved Jordan's ability to manage conflicts in other relationships, fostering a healthier approach to emotions and enhancing communication skills. The caring and understanding response from the caregiver not only resolved a single conflict but also equipped Jordan with the tools for better emotional regulation and problem-solving in the future.

Handling Adversity

Gaining insight into the neural bases of anger in adolescents not only sheds light on the intriguing realm of brain development, but also offers guidance during these challenging years. This emotional tempest will eventually pass, since this serves as a reminder. More complex and regulated expressions of rage are becoming possible as a result of brain evolution.

Being patient and compassionate is crucial for both the teenagers caught in the storm and those who are guiding them. Understanding that this extreme fury is a stage of growth that prepares one for emotional maturity is key. Teens can go through this tough time and come out stronger and smarter if we provide them with empathy, support, and ways to cope with these emotions. This effort is directly in conflict with the perceptions largely held about anger. Let's try and dispel some of them.

Common Misconceptions about Anger

Teens' anger is often unfairly criticized. Emotions are complicated and multi-facet ed, and they play a critical part in human growth. However, they are often portrayed as villains in stories about adolescence.

Addressing the misrepresentation and criticism of teenage anger requires a nuanced understanding of its role in development, and an acknowledgment of the often one-dimensional portrayal it receives in popular culture and media. Let's explore how this complex emotion is unjustly vilified, using examples from a book, a movie, and a piece of media commentary, followed by a reflection on real human experiences to debunk common myths about adolescent rage.

> Understanding the nuanced role of teenage anger requires debunking common misconceptions perpetuated by literature, film, media, and real-life experiences, where it's often unfairly criticized or misunderstood.

"The Catcher in the Rye" by J.D. Salinger

In the novel "The Catcher in the Rye," the protagonist, Holden Caulfield, embodies the misunderstood adolescent, navigating through the complexities of entering adulthood with a mixture of cynicism, sadness, and anger. Often, Holden's anger is criticized or dismissed by adults in the book, who see it as a phase or rebellion rather than a legitimate emotional response to his experiences and the phoniness he perceives in the adult world. This novel showcases how adolescent anger, when overlooked or misunderstood, can exacerbate feelings of isolation and misunderstanding.

"Inside Out"

"Inside Out," a Pixar film, personifies the emotions of Riley, an 11-year-old girl dealing with her family's move to a new city. Anger, one of the central characters, is initially portrayed as destructive and impulsive. However, as the story progresses, Anger's role is revealed to be crucial in protecting Riley's well-being and asserting her needs. This narrative shift highlights the importance of acknowledging and understanding anger as a necessary component of emotional health, rather than a villain to be suppressed.

Media Commentary

Media often highlights stories of teenage rebellion and conflict without providing the context of the underlying emotional struggles. For instance, news reports on teen protests or social media clashes might focus on the anger and confrontation aspects, labeling participants as overly emotional or irrational. This portrayal overlooks the legitimate grievances and the role of anger in driving social change, instead reinforcing stereotypes of teenage angst without acknowledging the positive attributes of passionate emotional expression.

Human Experience Reflection

Consider the experience of Maria, a 16-year-old who was frequently told her anger over societal injustices was just "teenage rebellion." When a teacher decided to channel Maria's anger into a project on social justice, Maria not only excelled but also inspired her peers to engage with issues they cared about. This experience demonstrates how recognizing and positively directing adolescent anger can lead to growth, engagement, and constructive outcomes, rather than conflict.

Let's shed light on the facts concerning adolescent rage and debunk some common fallacies.

Myth 1: Anger Can Never Be Positive and Helps Nothings

Anger is a natural and healthy emotion that every person experiences. This is a normal reaction to being wronged, having one's space invaded, or having one's values violated. The problem isn't anger per se, but rather the way it is channeled. When directed properly, anger has the power to inspire people to make amends, improve their communication skills, and establish healthy boundaries. The key is to channel the intensity of the present into a guiding light that shows the way forward.

Myth 2: Anger in Teens Is Always a Sign That Something Is Wrong

This misconception pigeonholes teenagers without taking into account the fact that puberty is inherently difficult. There is a great deal of personal, emotional, and social development during adolescence. Adolescents are figuring out who they are, how to fit in with their peers, and how to establish their individuality. Anger is not always a sign of a teenager's intrinsic lack of control or bad behavior, but rather a possible outcome of this hectic developmental phase. Now that we know this, we can help them deal with their anger in a healthy way by listening to them and offering them support.

Myth 3: you can't manage your anger by numbing or ignoring it.

If you want to learn how to control your anger, then you need to practice early signal recognition, identify what sets you off, and then figure out how to react constructively. Managing anger successfully entails expressing one's wants and emotions in a way that is forceful without being confrontational. Fostering more self-awareness and emotional intelligence may be achieved by encouraging teenagers to express the underlying emotions that accompany their anger, whether it fear, frustration, or pain.

When teenagers experience anger, it is often a surface reaction to deeper, more nuanced emotions. Encouraging them to explore and articulate these underlying feelings can be a powerful step toward emotional maturity and healthier interpersonal relationships. Here's a breakdown of how this process can unfold:

Identifying the Primary Emotion: Teach teenagers to pause and reflect on what they're feeling when anger surfaces. Is it really anger they're experiencing, or could it be fear of not being heard or understood? Perhaps it's frustration over situations that feel out of their control, or pain from feeling disregarded or disrespected.

Articulation of Emotions: Once the primary emotion is identified, the next step is to express it. This involves putting those feelings into words, which can be a challenge. Encouraging the use of "I feel" statements can be a helpful starting point. For example, "I feel frustrated when my opinions aren't considered" or "I feel hurt when I'm ignored."

Constructive Expression: Guide teenagers in expressing these emotions constructively. This means communicating their feelings in a way that is honest and vulnerable, yet respectful and non-accusatory. It's about sharing their internal emotional experience rather than focusing on the external actions or behaviors of others that triggered the anger.

Seeking Understanding and Resolution: The ultimate goal of expressing underlying emotions is to foster understanding and find a resolution that addresses the root cause of the anger. This might involve negotiating a compromise, establishing boundaries, or simply gaining a deeper mutual understanding of each other's perspectives.

Myth 4: Anger Problems Affect Just Specific Groups of Adolescents

In actuality, there is no correlation between one's socioeconomic level, standard of education, or background and the intensity of their anger. Any adolescent might have trouble controlling their anger, and everyone deals with anger in their own unique way. Some people express their anger via loud outbursts, while others may bottle it up and suffer from sadness or isolation. Adopting a more accepting and nurturing atmosphere for all adolescents requires first acknowledging that anger problems may impact everyone.

Expressing anger through loud outbursts or bottling it up can both be harmful, albeit in different ways, due to the negative repercussions on mental and emotional health, relationships, and overall well-being. Let's delve into why prolonging these behaviors can be problematic and the potential consequences.

Loud Outbursts

Loud, explosive expressions of anger can lead to several negative outcomes:

Damaged Relationships: Regular loud outbursts can strain or break personal and professional relationships. Friends, family members, and colleagues may feel frightened, hurt, or resentful, leading to distance or conflict.

Reputational Harm: Being known for uncontrollable anger can damage one's reputation, leading to social isolation or professional consequences, such as job loss or missed opportunities.

Physical Health Risks: Chronic anger and stress can increase the risk of health issues like heart disease, high blood pressure, insomnia, and a weakened immune system.

Emotional Exhaustion: Constantly managing the aftermath of outbursts can lead to feelings of guilt, regret, and emotional fatigue, impacting one's mental health.

Bottling Up Anger

Suppressing anger or internalizing it can also have detrimental effects:

Emotional and Physical Health: Long-term suppression of anger can contribute to anxiety, depression, and stress-related illnesses. Physical symptoms might include headaches, digestive issues, and sleep disturbances.

Passive-Aggressive Behavior: Bottling up anger often leads to passive-aggressive behavior, which can confuse and alienate others, leading to dysfunctional relationships.

Explosive Outbursts: Accumulated anger can eventually lead to explosive outbursts, which are often disproportionate to the triggering event and can cause significant damage to one's life and relationships.

Decreased Enjoyment of Life: Constantly suppressing emotions can lead to a diminished capacity to experience joy, satisfaction, and a sense of connection with others.

Why It's a Bad Thing: The Repercussions

Prolonging either behavior—explosive outbursts or bottling up anger—can lead to a cycle of emotional distress and interpersonal difficulties. In the case of loud outbursts, the immediate release of anger may provide a temporary sense of relief or power, but it's often followed by regret and a series of negative consequences that exacerbate stress and emotional turmoil.

Conversely, consistently suppressing anger denies the individual the opportunity to address and resolve underlying issues. It can lead to a build-up of unresolved emotions, which may manifest in harmful ways, either through physical symptoms, mental health issues, or eventual outbursts that are out of proportion to the cause.

Moreover, both patterns of dealing with anger prevent individuals from learning healthy coping mechanisms and effective communication skills. Without these skills, it's challenging to navigate conflicts constructively, advocate for one's needs, and build strong, supportive relationships.

Myth 5: Teen Anger Issues Can Be Resolved Through Time Alone

Teens' anger is often a symptom of deeper problems, and it's risky to assume that they will "grow out of" it. Without help, habits of ineffective anger control may persist into adulthood, impacting one's relationships, academic success, and mental health. Empowering youth to manage their emotions successfully requires proactive participation, which may be achieved via open communication, education, and, in some cases, professional help. This can promote resilience and emotional maturity.

Addressing teen anger through open communication, education, and, when necessary, professional help is crucial for fostering emotional resilience and maturity. Each of these strategies plays a vital role in equipping teens with the tools and understanding they need to manage their emotions constructively. Here's how these approaches can make a difference:

Open Communication

Open communication involves creating a safe and non-judgmental space where teens feel comfortable expressing their feelings and concerns. This approach helps in several ways:

Validation: It validates their feelings, making them feel heard and understood, which is fundamental for emotional well-being.

Problem-Solving: Through dialogue, teens can learn to articulate their problems and work collaboratively to find solutions, enhancing their problem-solving skills.

Trust Building: It strengthens trust between teens and their caregivers or mentors, important for fostering supportive relationships.

Education

Educating teens about emotions and anger management provides them with the knowledge to understand and navigate their feelings:

Self-awareness: Education helps teens recognize the signs of anger and understand its causes, leading to greater self-awareness and self-control.

Coping Strategies: It introduces healthy coping mechanisms, such as relaxation techniques, mindfulness, and assertive communication, offering alternatives to aggression or suppression.

Emotional Intelligence: Understanding emotions contributes to emotional intelligence, enabling teens to manage their feelings better and empathize with others.

Professional Help

In cases where teens struggle significantly with anger, professional help can be invaluable:

Tailored Support: Therapists can provide personalized strategies to address the root causes of anger, whether they stem from underlying mental health issues, trauma, or environmental factors.

Skill Development: Professional help often involves teaching emotional regulation skills and coping strategies in a structured way, ensuring teens have the resources to manage their anger effectively.

Family Involvement: Therapists can also work with families, teaching them how to support their teen's emotional development and manage conflict constructively at home.

Together, open communication, education, and professional intervention can significantly impact a teen's ability to handle anger. By addressing the issue from multiple angles, these strategies ensure that teens don't just "grow out" of their anger but rather grow through it, developing resilience and emotional maturity. This holistic approach can lead to improved relationships, academic success, and mental health, setting a foundation for a more balanced and fulfilling adult life.

The Influence of Context and Background

Environmental and experiential variables can impact our comprehension of adolescent rage. Part of how teenagers learn to manage their emotions is by imitating the actions of others around them at home, in the classroom, and in the community at large. Adolescents may learn to control their emotions by seeing and imitating adults who are able to do so in an accepting and safe setting.

Walking Side by Side

When dealing with angry teenagers, it's important to be patient, empathic, and communicative. Teens' emotional experiences are complicated, and by dispelling these beliefs, we are recognizing that. We are here to provide them with the necessary assistance throughout these challenging years while also offering advise that values their uniqueness.

Helping teenagers recognize and control their anger has long-term benefits. For a future filled with emotional intelligence and self-assurance, it paves the way. The narrative surrounding adolescent rage may be changed from a pessimistic one to a more positive one by empathy, persistence, and direction.

A Plea for Emotional Intelligence

In advocating for a shift in how we perceive and respond to adolescent anger, we're essentially calling for a deeper cultivation of emotional intelligence — both in ourselves as caregivers and within the teenagers we aim to support. Emotional intelligence, the ability to understand, use, and manage our own emotions in positive ways to relieve stress, communicate effectively, empathize with others, overcome challenges, and defuse conflict, serves as a crucial foundation for this transformation.

At its core, emotional intelligence involves four key skills:

Self-awareness: Recognizing one's own emotions and their effect on thoughts and behavior. This includes understanding triggers for anger and recognizing its impact.

Self-management: The ability to regulate emotions and behaviors in healthy ways, especially in stressful or challenging situations. This skill helps in choosing how to express anger constructively.

Social awareness: Understanding the emotions, needs, and concerns of others, building on empathy. It allows us to see beyond the surface of adolescent anger to the deeper issues or emotions that might be fueling it.

Relationship management: Developing and maintaining good relationships, communicating clearly, inspiring and influencing others, working well in a team, and managing conflict.

In short, Emotional intelligence allows one to keep a stable mental state, minimizing the tendencies to react aggressively. Emotionally intelligent people open up avenues for healthier expression and processing of this challenging emotion. They understand that it's not about suppressing anger but rather understanding its roots and transforming it into a constructive force. For teenagers, developing emotional intelligence means gaining the ability to navigate the complex feelings that accompany growing up without being overwhelmed by them.

The Role of Caregivers

For parents, teachers, and role models, enhancing our own emotional intelligence is just as important. It equips us to create environments where open communication is the norm, and education about emotions and how to handle them is integral. By embodying these principles, we can offer more empathetic support, guide teens through their emotional landscape, and help them build resilience and emotional maturity.

This approach to emotional intelligence emphasizes seeing anger not as a barrier but as an opportunity — to connect, understand, and guide. It's about creating spaces where adolescents feel seen and heard, where their emotions are validated, and where they are taught to navigate their feelings in ways that promote personal growth and stronger relationships. In doing so, we not only address the immediate challenges of adolescent anger but also lay the groundwork for emotionally intelligent future generations, capable of handling life's challenges with understanding and grace.

Key takeaways

- Teen anger is not a harmful force to be repressed, but rather a natural and healthy feeling that indicates underlying concerns or requirements.
- Teens' extreme anger is not a result of innate lack of control, but rather of continuous brain development and hormonal changes, especially in regions that are crucial for emotion regulation and impulse control.
- The key to effective anger management is not repressing but rather learning to identify and understand angry feelings and finding healthy methods to express them.
- Proactively addressing their anger with tolerance, empathy, and open communication, helps them develop healthier coping skills.
- Caregivers, teachers, and peers all have a part in setting a good example for adolescents when it comes to expressing and managing their emotions, including anger.

Summary of actionable steps

- **Consider Your Anger**
  Pause for a while and consider the things that cause you to get angry. Do you feel powerless generally or in response to a particular circumstance or person? The first stage in controlling your reaction is to identify these triggers.

- **Express your anger**
  Instead of repressing your anger, find a healthy way to express it. Some examples of this kind of activity include exercising, keeping a diary, or speaking to a reliable family member or friend. The

24

most important thing is to let your emotions flow freely without hurting yourself or others.

- **Cool down strategy**
  Find ways to relax when you're furious and include them into your cool-down strategy. Some effective techniques to allow yourself room to cool down include taking a few deep breaths, counting to 10, or moving away from the situation.

- **Speak Positively**
  Get in the habit of stating what you need and how you feel without being accusatory or aggressive. Express yourself using first-person "I" sentences; for example, "I feel upset when..."

- **Build an emotional vocabulary**
  After an outburst of rage, take note of what transpired and why; this will help you learn from your experience. Next time, think about how you may approach your emotions more constructively.

We have uncovered the complexity, dispelled the misconceptions, and understood the origins of adolescent rage; now it is time to go within. The following chapter, "Recognizing and Understanding Your Anger," will take us on an exploration of who we are. In the book, we will discover the indicators of mounting fury, how to pinpoint our own personal causes for it, and decipher the hidden meanings it conveys. If you want to learn how to see your emotional landscape with clarity, then this next chapter is for you.

CHAPTER 2

Recognizing and Understanding Your Anger

The greatest remedy for anger is delay.

– Seneca

ANGER, IN ITS essence, is a natural and universal emotion, experienced by all and indicative of our shared humanity. It arises in the face of perceived wrongs, injustice, or frustration. Yet, it is not the presence of anger that shapes our character or destiny, but our response to it. Seneca, a Stoic philosopher, offers timeless wisdom on the subject, suggesting that the space we create between feeling anger and acting on it can be our greatest tool in managing this powerful emotion.

When was the last time you were in the dryer and accidentally left a sock hanging out? I don't understand why this seemingly little thing is driving me crazy. Let your mind wander to a time when the sock stood in for your capacity to identify and comprehend your rage. The bigger battles with rage are often revealed by the little, apparently unimportant things that happen in our lives. Finding our metaphorical socks isn't the

> Understanding anger is akin to learning a new language—it empowers us to communicate effectively with ourselves and others, transforming conflict into opportunities for growth and connection.

only thing this chapter is about; it's also about discovering what makes us angry, where it comes from, and how to control it.

In this chapter, we probe into the landscape of anger, exploring its many contours and the paths it may lead us down. Understanding anger is akin to learning a new language — it allows us to communicate more effectively with ourselves and others, transforming potential conflict into opportunities for growth and connection. By recognizing the early signs of anger and approaching it with introspection and purpose, we can navigate our emotions in a way that reflects our deepest values and aspirations.

Before you begin your anger management process, remember that anger does not define you. Your power lies in your ability to recognize, understand, and channel your anger into actions that speak to who you truly are and who you aspire to be.

At its core, anger is a signal. When our wants aren't satisfied, our boundaries are violated, or our values are questioned, it sends a signal. But amid the chaos of adolescence, its meanings may easily be misunderstood. To help you react in a manner that reflects your best self, this chapter will teach you how to decipher the language of rage and grasp its real meanings.

Are you prepared to face your anger head-on and learn about yourself? As we go further, keep in mind that knowing your anger is a powerful tool for managing it gracefully and powerfully. Together, let's start this crucial task and turn the page.

Identifying Common Anger Triggers in Teens

Understanding what sparks anger in young adults is like looking to decode a complex language without a translator. It's a difficult mission, given that those years are packed with fast modifications, intense feelings, and the quest for identity. Let's gently peel back the layers to expose some of the typical situations or events that frequently mildens the fuse of stripling anger, aiming to technique those revelations with warmth and knowledge.

Feeling Like You're Not Being Heard or Understood

Imagine seeking to voice complex issues central to you, only to feel like you are talking into the void. For many young adults, the experience of now not being heard or feeling misunderstood by parents, teachers, or even buddies can be especially irritating. It's like shouting into a wind tunnel, wherein your phrases get muffled in the noise. This battle for voice and validation subsequently spiral into feelings of anger and isolation.

The Pressure Cooker of Peer Influence

Adolescents face immense pressure in their daily lives that directly comes from the people who surrounded them. The desire to be in shape, to be accepted, and to meet the myriad unstated requirements of one's peers can be arduous and tension-inducing. Teens might go through a range of intense emotions, including rage and resentment when they feel pressured to conform or remain the same because of expectations that don't match their true selves. It feels like you need to take off a saggy mask; it's unpleasant.

The Weight of the World

There's a heavy burden that incorporates the expectancy to excel academically and make definitive life choices about one's future. This stress, whether it comes from inside, from mother and father, or from society, can create a cauldron of stress. When teens sense that they're continuously being measured and determined wanting, or when the path beforehand seems impossibly slim, it may ignite a firestorm of anger and frustration. It's like being in a race wherein the finish line keeps pushing further away.

The Tug-of-War of Family Dynamics

Family lifestyles, with all its complexities, may be a significant source of emotional turmoil for teens. Conflicts with dad and mom over independence, disagreements with siblings, or navigating through circle of relatives' upheavals, like divorce, can fire up a maelstrom of emotions, with anger frequently at the leading edge. It's akin to playing a function in a play where the script keeps converting, and no one gave you the today's version.

The Sting of Injustice

As teens shape their personal views on right and wrong, experiences of injustice, whether private or discovered, can deeply affect them. Discrimination, bullying, or witnessing unfair treatment can catalyze a robust response, wherein anger turns into both a defence and a sword. It's a reaction to the sector's harshness, a manner of saying, "This is not okay."

Peeling back the layers of teenage anger reveals common triggers like feeling unheard, peer pressure, academic stress, family dynamics, and experiences of injustice, each igniting a firestorm of frustration and resentment in young adults striving to find their voice and identity.

The Heartache of Young Love

Navigating romantic relationships for the first time may be like cruising uncharted waters — exciting but additionally fraught with risk. The depth of first loves, coupled with the pain of heartbreak or jealousy, may be overwhelming. Teens learn to control a storm of current emotions, including fury, via these tales, which are about more than simply the relationships themselves.

The Whirlwind of Hormonal Changes

Puberty isn't only a bodily transformation, but an emotional overhaul as well. The hormonal modifications that accompany this degree of existence could make feelings feel bigger and further uncontrollable. It's as if someone turned up the volume on your feelings without consulting you first.

Recognizing and understanding these triggers is like locating a map in a dense woodland — it doesn't at once alternate the landscape, but it does offer a process toward that end.

The Role of Peer Pressure and Social Media

As you make your way through adolescence, you'll encounter new obstacles at every turn, like you're in a never-ending labyrinth. Peer pressure and the impact of social media are two of the most significant obstacles that kids face nowadays. Feelings of rage, frustration, and isolation may be amplified when these elements come together to form a distinct environment. Let's explore how these factors interact to shape the emotional world of modern teenagers.

Peer Pressure

Envision yourself in a room full of people who seem to have no idea where they are meant to be, except for you. Peer pressure might seem like that at times. It's not necessarily about being forced to do something you don't want to do; sometimes it's the unspoken pressure to conform, whether that's via what you dress, the music you listen to, or even your ideas. It may be draining to feel this hidden pressure to conform to the standards set by your peers.

A major cause of resentment for many teenagers is the struggle to be yourself while yet being accepted. It's as if you're in the middle of a frustrating tug-of-war and you can never be sure of where you stand. A common outward sign of this inner turmoil is rage, directed at oneself for capitulating, one's peers for applying unseen pressure, and the society at large for instituting these norms.

The Intersection of Social Media and Peer Pressure

Peer pressure and social media have come together to form a powerful combination of factors that may provoke emotions. One side of the coin is that social media may make peer pressure seem even more pervasive. On the other side, it may enable bullying in a roundabout way, rumors to fly about, and passive-aggressive conduct, all of which can set rage ablaze.

As they try to find their place in the world, teenagers may feel pressured to conform to an idealized version of themselves by compromising on their hobbies, looks, and even their views. Anger and irritation might set in when there's a stark contrast between their true selves and the image they believe others expect of them. As people participate more, the pressure mounts, and their emotional responses get more intense—it's a self-perpetuating loop.

Challenging Conditions

The first step in addressing adolescent aggression is to have a better understanding of how peer pressure and social media contribute to this problem. Building good coping skills, engaging in self-reflection, and having open conversations are all steps on the path to managing these emotions. A way out of the storm may be found by encouraging kids to speak about what they've been through, to question the pressures they're under, and to investigate the feelings that lie underneath their fury.

> Peer pressure and social media amplify teenage rage, creating a complex emotional landscape that demands understanding and coping strategies for adolescents navigating these challenges.

Assisting kids in understanding that their value isn't contingent on social media likes, shares, or peer acceptance is the main goal. It's important to help children realize that it's normal to disconnect from social media when it becomes too much, to appreciate their uniqueness, and to go inside for reinforcement. The most important thing is that kids should know that they are not alone in experiencing these emotions; that they are part of a common fight, but that it should not define their adolescence. Such a support must come from the inside the place they call their home, which we will discuss next.

Count To Ten

Count to ten (or even twenty) before reacting to a situation. This brief pause allows time for emotions to settle and for rational thinking to take over, preventing impulsive reactions.

Family Dynamics and Its Influence

Family is the most fundamental unit in the complex web of human connections; it is through them that we learn to manage our emotions, resolve conflicts, and express ourselves in the first place. When it comes to the unpredictable feeling of rage, it is crucial for teens to comprehend the complex relationships within their families as they navigate the turbulent seas of puberty. Join me as I explore the intricate web of family dynamics and how they impact rage in teenagers.

The Emotional Crucible

The term "emotional crucible" is often used metaphorically to describe a situation or period in life that involves significant emotional stress or challenge, which, like a crucible in metallurgy where substances are heated to very high temperatures to induce a chemical change, leads to transformation or growth. This concept can be applied in various contexts, including personal development, therapy, and relationship dynamics.

In personal development, an emotional crucible can refer to a deeply challenging experience that forces an individual to confront and work through difficult emotions, leading to personal growth and increased emotional resilience. These experiences often push individuals to their emotional limits but also offer profound opportunities for learning about oneself, re-evaluating life priorities, and developing new coping mechanisms.

In therapy and psychological contexts, the term may be used to describe intense therapeutic processes or relationships that challenge clients to confront and resolve deep-seated emotional issues. The therapist-client relationship itself can become an emotional crucible, providing a safe space for the client to explore and understand their emotions, behaviors, and thought patterns, leading to transformational change.

In the context of relationship dynamics, especially in couples' therapy, an emotional crucible can refer to a phase where partners face and work through significant conflicts or challenges. This process, while often difficult, can lead to deeper intimacy and understanding, as partners learn to navigate their differences and vulnerabilities together.

The concept of the emotional crucible underscores the idea that while intense emotional experiences can be challenging, they also hold the potential for profound personal growth and transformation.

Top of Form

Emotions like happiness, sorrow, fear, and rage are initially shaped in the context of family, where they become an integral part of who we are. Our ability to interpret our caregivers' emotional signals begins at birth and forms the foundation of our own emotional intelligence. Anger takes form in this furnace, shaped by the ways those closest to us react and respond.

Adolescents develop constructive coping mechanisms for anger management in homes where adults are supportive, understanding, and communicative. Because they know they will be understood and supported, kids are able to open up about how they are feeling. Teens may internalize their emotions and keep them bottled up if they grow up in an atmosphere where they are mocked, dismissed, or otherwise treated hostilely.

A Conflict Tapestry

The ups and downs of family life create complex patterns of interaction, including conflict, which shapes adolescents' understanding and expression of anger. Teens may learn a lot about emotional control, negotiation, and compromise from examples of healthy conflict resolution. Teens learn to control their anger in healthy ways when they grow up in homes that address problems with compassion, dignity, and a commitment to finding solutions.

"The way conflict is handled within families significantly influences how adolescents perceive and express anger. Healthy conflict resolution fosters emotional control, negotiation, and compromise, while unhealthy dynamics can lead to increased emotional distress and resorting to violent responses."

Teens may find it difficult to control their anger if they grow up in homes where arguments are either ignored, repressed, or responded to violently. They could experience increased emotional discomfort due to feelings of being ignored, invalidated, or helpless. The other extreme is when they resort to violent methods of resolving conflicts, which only serves to fuel other episodes of hostility.

Do You Prescribe a Nurturing Approach to Parenting or a Method for Handling Conflict?

Parenting styles are fundamental to family dynamics and have a distinct impact on adolescents' anger management skills. Children with authoritative parents are more likely to develop emotional regulation skills when they are warm, have firm limits set for them, and are encouraged to talk about their feelings. Anger is a normal feeling, they learn, and they can control it by talking things out and finding solutions.

On the other side, teens may learn to repress their anger under authoritarian parents that place an excessive focus on control and compliance. A powder keg of suppressed rage may be created when people avoid showing their true feelings for fear of rejection or punishment. Conversely, even if they mean well, parents who are too liberal with their teenagers may not provide them the framework they need to manage their emotions.

Interactive Activities to Identify Personal Triggers

Adolescents experience a wide range of emotions, and rage is definitely one among them. But have no fear; we can learn to manage our anger in better and more constructive ways with the help of self-awareness and a toolbox of coping techniques.

Keeping a Record of Things That Make You Anger

To begin, I propose the Anger Trigger Journal, an exercise that is both easy to do and full of useful information. Visualize yourself in a quiet place where you may let your emotions and ideas flow freely whenever frustration strikes. Take out your reliable diary and begin penning your thoughts whenever that all-too-familiar wave of irritation washes over you. Think on what happened, what feelings were running through your body, and how you handled the scenario that made you angry. We may

35

learn a lot about our emotional landscape and the patterns that lead to our rage if we keep track of these instances.

Investigating Triggers

Now is the perfect opportunity to tap into our inner Sherlock Holmes as we engage in the Trigger Detective exercise. Picture this: we get a deck of mystery cards, and each one represents a potential trigger. These cards cover the whole spectrum of adolescent distress, from arguments between siblings to peer pressure and academic strain. It is up to us now to imagine ourselves in the protagonist's position and practice our reactions to each possible circumstance. We may improve our problem-solving abilities and build a toolbox of healthy coping mechanisms by putting ourselves in the shoes of other people and trying out different reactions.

The Mystery of the Midnight Message

Imagine you draw a card from the deck titled "The Mystery of the Midnight Message." This card describes a scenario where the protagonist, Jordan, receives a cryptic and somewhat negative text message from a friend right before bedtime. The message is vague but seems to hint at disappointment or anger towards Jordan. This situation becomes our focus as we step into Jordan's shoes to unravel the mystery and manage the emotional triggers it presents.

Identifying the Trigger

First, we identify the potential triggers in this scenario:

Uncertainty: The ambiguity of the message's content can lead to overthinking and anxiety.

Assumption of Negative Intent: Without clear communication, there's a tendency to assume the worst about the message's tone and content.

Fear of Conflict or Loss: Concern that this message might indicate a serious issue or the potential loss of a friendship.

Vanquishing the Trigger

Next, we strategize healthy ways to address and overcome these triggers:

Seek Clarification: Instead of stewing in uncertainty and possibly worsening our emotional state, we decide to communicate directly with the friend. However, given the late hour, we resolve to wait until the morning, recognizing the importance of addressing such matters at a more appropriate time.

Manage Initial Reactions: In the meantime, we practice calming techniques to manage our emotional response. This could involve deep breathing, writing down our feelings and possible responses, or engaging in a brief distraction to calm down, like reading a book or listening to music.

Prepare for Constructive Conversation: We plan out how to approach the conversation in a non-confrontational way, focusing on expressing our feelings about the message and asking for clarity. The goal is to understand the intent behind the message without assuming negativity or escalating the situation.

Reflecting on the Outcome

By morning, after some rest and with a clearer mind, Jordan reaches out to the friend. It turns out the message was sent in frustration over a separate issue and wasn't intended to be hurtful or cryptic. The friend apologizes for the late-night message, and they discuss better ways to communicate in the future.

Through this exercise, we've not only navigated a common adolescent trigger but also practiced essential skills in emotional regulation, communication, and problem-solving. By stepping into Jordan's shoes, we gain insight into the complexity of triggers and the power of proactive, positive response strategies.

Mental Diary

Using the Thought Tracker, let's change our attention to the influence of our thoughts. Envision a table with columns marking various stages of our anger management process. We will use this worksheet to document our thoughts and feelings in a comprehensive manner whenever anger arises. Let's record what started us off, break down the first ideas that came to mind, explore the feelings that swirled about, and record our response. We may learn a great deal about our own thinking processes and behavioral habits as we follow the path of our anger, which will lead to personal development and progress.

Visualizing the Thought Tracker: A Step-by-Step Guide

Imagine a straightforward table or worksheet designed to dissect and understand your anger episodes. This table is divided into four main columns, each serving a specific purpose in your journey to manage anger more effectively. Here's how to visualize and utilize it:

1. Trigger Event:

Column Label: Trigger
Description: This column is for noting down the specific event or situation that sparked your anger. It could be anything from a disagreement with a friend to receiving a low grade on a test.
Example Entry: Argument with my sibling over sharing the computer.

2. Initial Thoughts:

Column Label: Thoughts
Description: Here, you record the first thoughts that crossed your mind when you felt anger bubbling up. These thoughts often frame how we perceive the trigger event.
Example Entry: "They always get their way, and I'm left out."

3. Emotions and Feelings:

Column Label: Emotions

Description: This column is dedicated to identifying and naming the emotions and feelings that arose following the initial thoughts. Anger often masks other feelings, so being specific is key.

Example Entry: Frustration, injustice, feeling undervalued.

4. Response and Outcome:

Column Label: Response

Description: The final column is for reflecting on how you responded to the feelings of anger and the outcome of that response. Did it escalate the situation, or did you find a way to calm down?

Example Entry: Yelled and stormed off, leading to a longer-lasting argument.

Using the Thought Tracker

By filling out this table each time you experience anger, you can start to see patterns in your triggers, thoughts, and reactions. Over time, you'll identify common themes and learn how your initial thoughts can shape your emotional responses. This awareness is the first step toward choosing different, more constructive responses to anger in the future.

For instance, if you notice that feeling undervalued is a common theme in your emotional responses, you might work on assertiveness techniques or discuss your feelings in a calm moment to address this recurring issue.

Anger Log

Now, let's take a trip down memory lane with the Anger Timeline exercise. Imagine a path for your anger that begins with the incident that sets it off and continues through your emotional landscape until it reaches its final destination. By keeping track of our emotions, ideas, and deeds at each step, we may trace the development of our rage. Making a mental picture of our anger management steps may help us see trends, zero in on problem areas, and get insight into how our emotions play out.

Here we have it — a wealth of engaging exercises aimed at revealing the secrets of what makes us angry. Let us not forget that the first step towards conquering our anger is to understand it as we begin this path of self-discovery and progress. We will face the challenges of puberty head-on, but we will emerge from it stronger and wiser than before.

Key takeaways

- Situations, ideas, emotions, and bodily sensations may all serve as triggers for anger, albeit they might differ from one individual to the next.
- If we want to learn how to control our anger, we need to know what makes us angry in the first place.
- Because of the ways in which social media and peer pressure shape our opinions, actions, and reactions, anger management problems may become even more severe.

Summary of actionable steps

If you want to know how you react emotionally and behaviorally when you're angry, it could help to draw a picture of your rage trip from beginning to end.

You may become more self-aware, learn healthy coping mechanisms, and overcome your anger triggers by making five simple changes to your everyday routine. Always keep in mind that becoming better at controlling your anger is a process, and that progress toward emotional health and self-improvement is incremental.

In the coming chapter, we will unpack the ways in which our physiology and psychology structure our experience of anger. From the adrenaline rush that accompanies heightened motivation to the complex emotional mechanisms underpinning our emotional responses, we will unlock the inner workings of anger and equip it with valuable knowledge and insight in ourselves to meet its challenges successfully.

Join me as we set out to explore the dynamic relationship between our physical states and our emotional experiences. Together, we will gain a deeper understanding of anger and discover practical ways to deal with it effectively. By delving into the physical and emotional state of anger, we will pave the way for greater self-awareness and emotional well-being.

CHAPTER 3

The Physical and Emotional Landscape of Anger

> *Anger is an acid that can do more harm to the vessel in which it is stored than to anything on which it is poured.*
>
> – Mark Twain

PICTURE YOURSELF IN a situation where visceral emotions like rage were overwhelming. A strong emotion, anger may sweep over us like a tempest, impacting our physical and emotional health. This chapter will explore the complex link between the physical and emotional components of rage, specifically how they interact with each other to create our unique perception of this powerful emotion.

Some of the topics we will discuss are as follows:

- The physical manifestations of anger, such as a racing heart, red cheeks, and the adrenaline rush that makes us ready to act.
- Rather than existing in a vacuum, anger often interacts with a wide range of other emotions, including fear, sorrow, resentment, and frustration. We'll take a look at the ways in which these emotions may impact and be affected by rage.
- Anger management success hinges on being able to see the precursors of a furious outburst. We will talk about the signs

that people often show when their anger is getting out of hand and how to stop it from becoming worse.

Come with us as we delve into the depths of fury, discovering its emotional complexities and physical expressions. We may learn to control our anger and improve our emotional health by understanding the intricate relationship between our thoughts and bodies.

Understanding the Physiology of Anger

Understanding the physiology of anger involves recognizing the immediate reactions within our body, as well as acknowledging the long-term health implications of frequent or chronic anger. Anger initiates a cascade of physiological changes, often referred to as the "fight or flight" response, preparing the body to either face a perceived threat or flee from it. This response includes the release of stress hormones such as adrenaline and cortisol, increased heart rate, elevated blood pressure, and heightened alertness. While these reactions are designed to protect us in acute situations, the long-term effects of sustained or frequent anger can be detrimental to our health.

Case Example

John, a 45-year-old executive, experienced frequent bouts of anger at work. Over the years, this chronic stress began to take a toll on his health. Initially, John noticed an increase in headaches and difficulty sleeping. Over time, during a routine check-up, his doctor diagnosed him with hypertension, a condition he hadn't previously had. John's family history of heart disease, coupled with his high-stress lifestyle and frequent anger, put him at significant risk for cardiovascular complications. Following his diagnosis, John decided to seek help for anger management. Through therapy and stress reduction techniques, such as mindfulness and exercise, John learned healthier ways to process and express his emotions. Over the following year, not only did his blood pressure improve, but he also reported feeling less stressed and more in control of his emotions, illustrating the profound impact that managing anger can have on physical health.

Understanding the physiology of anger and recognizing the long-term effects on health is crucial. By addressing anger and learning effective management strategies, individuals can significantly improve their physical and mental well-being, enhancing their quality of life.

The Sympathetic Nervous System in Action

As soon as our bodies detect danger, the sympathetic nervous system goes into overdrive. This vital part of our autonomic nervous system coordinates the fight-or-flight reaction, getting us ready to either face the danger directly or run away. When this system is activated, our bodies undergo a sequence of changes that make us more physically prepared to take action.

The Secretion of Stress Chemicals

The quick secretion of adrenaline and cortisol, two stress chemicals, is fundamental to the physiological reaction of rage. The release of these powerful substances into our circulation triggers the activation of our bodies' defense mechanisms. Cortisol heightens alertness and energy levels, but adrenaline quickens our pulse rate, raises blood pressure, and sharpens our senses. Our bodies are physically prepared to face or flee from the object of our wrath as a result of this hormonal surge.

Pain, Stiffness, and Other Physical Symptoms

At the same time as our bodies react to anger, we experience a cascade of bodily sensations that are easy to recognize. As our bodies get ready for a violent confrontation, we clench our teeth, tighten our muscles, and our fists may unconsciously ball up. As our level of excitement rises, our breathing becomes shallow and quick. These physical changes occur when our bodies are getting ready to deal with the injustice or danger that made us angry in the first place.

Effects on Brain Function

Our brain's emotional center, the amygdala, is especially vulnerable to the destructive effects of rage due to its complex neural architecture. The amygdala goes into overdrive when we're angry, mistaking environmental cues for danger and setting off a cascade of stress hormone releases. Our capacity to think clearly and react calmly to the issue at hand might be impaired when our amygdala activity is heightened, hijacking our logical thinking processes. Consequently, our heightened emotional state can cause us to behave hastily or unreasonably.

Overt Expressions of Aggression

In addition to the physiological changes that occur inside our bodies, there are also evident external manifestations of rage. We may often tell how we're feeling by our flushed skin, perspiration, shaking, or tightened jaw. People around us may see the severity of our emotions and the possibility of an escalation via these bodily signals that indicate how angry we are.

Impact on Health in the Long Run

Appetite for wrath is fleeting, but our physical well-being might take a hit if it goes unchecked for too long. A number of health problems, including hypertension, heart disease, impaired immunological function, and even accelerated aging, have been associated to chronic rage. It is crucial to learn effective ways to deal with and control this intense emotion, especially in light of the possible long-term effects of repressed rage.

Did You Know?

Approximately 64% of young people (from 14 to 21 years old) experience uncontrolled anger.

Linking Anger with Emotional Responses

The complex range of human feeling is enhanced by the complex web of relationships between different states of mind, one of them being anger. Investigating the interplay between rage and other emotions reveals the far-reaching effects it has on our mental health and relationships with others.

How Other Emotions Interact

Rather than being in a static state, anger is always a part of a complex web of emotions, with one feeling amplifying and impacting the others. Anger may be amplified and shaped by other negative emotions such as resentment, fear, melancholy, or guilt.

Imagine Sarah, a high school student who has been struggling with her grades. Recently, she received a lower-than-expected score on an important test, a situation that initially sparked frustration and disappointment. These feelings quickly turned into resentment towards her teacher, whom she felt didn't provide adequate support or resources.

Exploring the interconnectedness of anger with other emotions illuminates its profound impact on mental health and interpersonal relationships.

As the days passed, this resentment mixed with a growing sense of fear about her future academic prospects and guilt over not having studied more effectively.

One afternoon, Sarah's younger brother accidentally knocked over a cup of water onto her study notes. This minor incident, which might have elicited a mild annoyance under different circumstances, instead triggered an intense reaction from Sarah. She lashed out at her brother with disproportionate anger, surprising even herself.

Upon reflection, Sarah recognized that her reaction wasn't just about the spilled water; it was the culmination of a series of compounded emotions. Her underlying fear about her academic future and the guilt she felt over her study habits intensified her anger towards an unintended target. Recognizing this web of emotions, Sarah decided to seek support. She talked to her teacher about her concerns, opened up to her parents about her fears, and started working with a tutor to improve her study habits. By addressing the root causes of her anger and the intertwined emotions, Sarah found healthier ways to cope and gradually felt more in control of her reactions.

Effects on the Control of Emotions

Anger may make it very difficult to manage our emotions, which in turn makes it hard to think rationally and exercise self-control. Irrational decision-making, impulsive actions, and trouble controlling emotions might result from our cognitive processes being warped when we are gripped by rage. As a result, people may find it difficult to handle difficult circumstances or express their emotions in a healthy way, which may worsen emotional pain and interpersonal conflicts.

Adaptive and Maladaptive Strategies for Dealing with Stress

In order to manage the emotional distress caused by excessive anger, people may turn to a variety of coping techniques. Seeking out social support or practicing relaxation methods are examples of adaptive coping mechanisms; on the other hand, there are also maladaptive measures that may lead to an endless loop of emotional distress. Substance misuse, aggressiveness, or avoidance behaviors are examples of maladaptive coping techniques that might alleviate anger in the short term, but they do nothing to resolve the emotional pain and interpersonal conflicts that stem from these actions.

Effects on Personal Connections

The way we express and control our anger greatly influences the strength of our relationships with others. Neglecting to address anger may put a burden on relationships, damage trust, and weaken intimacy, ultimately resulting in animosity, resentment, and emotional withdraw. In addition, unfavorable interpersonal dynamics and ineffective communication and problem-solving may result from uncontrolled rage. Relationships based on mutual respect and understanding are more likely to be peaceful and helpful if people learn to express their emotions in a healthy way and know how to resolve conflicts.

Understanding the impact of trauma on the brain is crucial for recognizing why individuals may react differently to similar situations. Trauma can significantly alter the brain's response to stress, often leading to heightened sensitivity to perceived threats and a more intense or prolonged emotional reaction. Here's an example comparing the reactions of two individuals—one with a trauma-induced brain and another more in control of their emotions—to the same stressful situation.

> Understanding trauma's impact on the brain helps recognize varied reactions to stress, crucial for effective conflict resolution.

Situation

During a team meeting at work, a manager critiques a project proposal presented by two team members, Alex (who has a history of trauma) and Jordan (who has developed strong emotional regulation skills).

Reaction of Emir (Trauma-Induced Brain)

For Emir, the manager's critique triggers an immediate and intense stress response. The brain's amygdala, hyper-vigilant due to past trauma, perceives the critique not as constructive feedback but as a direct threat. This activates the fight-or-flight response, leading to a rapid release of stress hormones, which escalates Emir's emotional state. Instead of focusing on the content of the feedback, Emir feels personally attacked, resulting in either a defensive outburst ("This isn't fair! You don't understand the work I put into this!") or a complete shutdown, withdrawing from the meeting and struggling to communicate effectively. This reaction is less about the present critique and more about a past pattern of threat response etched into Emir's brain by trauma.

Reaction of john (More in Control of Emotions)

John, on the other hand, perceives the same critique through a different lens. With a prefrontal cortex well-practiced in emotional regulation, John is able to pause and process the manager's comments without immediate emotional escalation. This pause allows for a reasoned assessment of the feedback's validity and relevance. John acknowledges the emotional sting of criticism but views it as an opportunity for growth, responding with a calm request for specific suggestions ("I understand the concerns. Could you provide more detailed feedback to help us improve?"). For John, the critique is a professional interaction, not a personal attack.

Comparative Analysis

The key difference in reactions between Emir and john can be attributed to the varying impacts of trauma and emotional regulation skills on brain function. Trauma can sensitize the brain to perceive threat where there is none, triggering disproportionate emotional and physiological responses. In contrast, strong emotional regulation skills, which can be developed over time through various practices and

49

therapies, enable an individual to interpret situations more objectively and respond in a measured way.

Evaluating Things Cognitively and Emotionally

Anger is only one of many emotional reactions that might result from how we choose to perceive the world around us. Some cognitive distortions that may lead to distorted views and heightened anger in reaction to perceived injustices or dangers include personalizing, black-and-white thinking, and catastrophizing. In addition, our cognitive evaluation of events is shaped by our prior experiences, beliefs, and cultural norms, which in turn affect the strength and length of our angry reactions.

Cognitive distortions are irrational or exaggerated thought patterns that can lead to negative emotions, including anger. These distortions affect how we interpret events, interactions, and the world around us, often leading to emotional distress and behavioral issues. By understanding these distortions, such as personalizing, black-and-white thinking, and catastrophizing, we can begin to see how they create biases and blocks in our daily lives.

Personalizing

Personalizing is a cognitive distortion where an individual interprets unrelated or loosely related events as having direct significance to themselves, often assuming blame for situations outside their control.

When someone personalizes events, they may feel an undue sense of responsibility or guilt for things that are not their fault. This can lead to heightened anger, especially if they perceive themselves as constantly at fault or victimized by others' actions.

If a friend cancels plans, someone prone to personalizing might think, "They canceled because they don't enjoy spending time with me," rather than considering other reasons unrelated to them. This can lead to feelings of anger and resentment towards the friend, damaging the relationship over perceived slights that are not intentional or personal.

Black-and-White Thinking

Black-and-white thinking, also known as all-or-nothing thinking, involves seeing things in extreme, either/or categories without acknowledging any middle ground or gray areas.

This type of thinking can lead to rigid expectations and a lack of flexibility in understanding others' behaviors and motives. It can amplify feelings of anger when reality does not align with these binary expectations.

A student who gets a B on a test and thinks, "If I'm not perfect, I've failed," may experience significant anger and frustration. This binary viewpoint blocks the ability to see the positive aspects of their performance and can create unnecessary emotional turmoil.

Catastrophizing

Catastrophizing involves expecting the worst possible outcome in a situation, often blowing potential problems out of proportion.

This distortion can cause intense emotional reactions to relatively minor events, as the individual anticipates disaster or extreme negative consequences. The anticipation of these outcomes can provoke severe anxiety and anger when faced with everyday challenges.

If someone hears rumors of layoffs at work, catastrophizing might lead them to immediately assume they'll be fired, leading to anger and stress about perceived injustice or betrayal by the employer. This may cause unnecessary tension and conflict in the workplace, even if their job was never at risk.

Overcoming Cognitive Distortions

Recognizing and challenging these cognitive distortions is crucial for emotional regulation and healthier interpersonal interactions. Techniques like cognitive-behavioral therapy (CBT) can help individuals identify their distorted thought patterns, understand their impacts, and develop more balanced and rational ways of interpreting events. By addressing these biases and blocks, individuals can reduce unnecessary anger and improve their day-to-day emotional resilience and wellbeing.

Emotional Regulation and Healthy Expression

Improving one's ability to control and express emotions is crucial for healthy anger management and emotional development. People may learn to control their emotions, lower their physiological arousal, and develop adaptive coping mechanisms via cognitive-behavioral tactics, relaxation methods, and mindfulness practices. Conflict resolution and improved interpersonal connections are additional benefits of developing empathy, compassion, and confident communication abilities. Anger and other emotions may be better managed with self-awareness and resilience when people have a more comprehensive view of emotional health. This, in turn, leads to happier, more satisfying lives.

Understanding the interconnected nature of rage and other emotions sheds light on the complexity of being human. Developing emotional intelligence, being self-aware, and developing good coping strategies allow people to tap into the transforming power of emotions, leading to improved well-being and harmonious relationships.

We rarely ever begin our anger at the zenith. There is a domino-effect which builds our emotions into explosive anger.

Incorporating precise clarity about emotional regulation, particularly through the lens of trauma-informed studies and understanding the neurological processes involved, can significantly enhance the depth and applicability of this topic. To meet this need, let's delve into the neurological underpinnings of emotional regulation and highlight how trauma can affect these processes, alongside presenting cognitive-behavioral strategies and mindfulness practices with a focus on empirical research findings.

Neurological Processes in Emotional Regulation

Emotional regulation involves several key areas of the brain, including the prefrontal cortex (PFC), the amygdala, and the hippocampus. The PFC, responsible for executive functions such as planning, decision-making, and impulse control, plays a crucial role in regulating emotions by moderating the amygdala's response to stress and emotional stimuli. The amygdala, often referred to as the brain's "alarm system," processes emotional responses, especially fear and anger. The hippocampus is involved in forming memories, including the contextual understanding of emotions.

Impact of Trauma on Emotional Regulation

Trauma can significantly disrupt these neurological processes. Research indicates that exposure to trauma, especially during critical developmental periods, can lead to heightened amygdala reactivity and diminished PFC regulation. This imbalance often results in an increased stress response and difficulty managing emotions, a condition known as emotional dysregulation. Moreover, changes in the hippocampus due to trauma can affect how emotional memories are processed and recalled, complicating emotional responses to new stimuli.

Cognitive-Behavioral Tactics and Mindfulness Practices

Cognitive-behavioral therapy (CBT) has been shown to be effective in addressing emotional dysregulation by helping individuals reframe negative thought patterns that exacerbate emotional responses (Beck, 2011). Through CBT, individuals learn to identify cognitive distortions and apply more adaptive thinking, which can reduce the intensity and frequency of anger outbursts.

Mindfulness practices, including meditation and mindful breathing, have been found to enhance emotional regulation by increasing awareness of emotional states and reducing reactivity. A study by Tang et al. (2015) demonstrated that mindfulness training could strengthen the connectivity between the PFC and the amygdala, improving the capacity for emotional regulation.

Developing Empathy, Compassion, and Communication

Skills

Empathy and compassion training, often integrated into therapeutic approaches like Dialectical Behavior Therapy (DBT), can further support emotional regulation by fostering a deeper understanding of others' emotions and perspectives, which, in turn, can enhance interpersonal relationships and reduce conflict. Skills in assertive communication, a focus of both CBT and DBT, enable individuals to express their needs and emotions constructively, without resorting to aggression or passivity.

Recognizing the Signs of Escalating Anger

Anger is a normal human emotion, but it may quickly turn from mild irritation to full-blown wrath. In order to control this powerful emotion and avoid negative consequences, it is essential to know how to notice the warning signals of anger building up. People may learn to regulate their anger before it gets out of hand by being more self-aware and paying attention to a variety of signals, including those that are physical, mental, behavioral, verbal, emotional, and environmental.

Signs on the Body

When anger levels rise, people could feel a variety of bodily feelings. Some of these symptoms may include a racing heart, shallow breathing, tense muscles, clenched fists, and a reddening of the face. Understanding the physiological reaction of the body to anger and being able to recognize these signs early on may help you intervene before your emotions get the best of you.

Cognitive Distortions

When we're angry, our thoughts tend to be skewed, which makes us feel even worse. Anger may escalate when people think in absolute terms, make hasty judgments, generalize too much, or focus too much on themselves. Anger may spiral out of control if people don't learn to recognize their own cognitive distortions and question their own illogical beliefs.

Alterations in Behaviour

Changes in conduct are often seen as anger levels rise. Anxiety, pacing, and fidgeting are some of the ways these symptoms could appear. People may become violent in severe instances, acting out in ways like yelling, gesturing threateningly, or even being physically violent. Individuals may actively de-escalate and avoid future escalation of situations by recognizing these behavioral signs.

The Spectrum of Anger Manifestations

Anger is a multifaceted emotion that spans a broad spectrum, from mild irritation to intense fury, and it can manifest in both overt and covert behaviors. Beyond the visible signs like yelling or physical aggression, there are subtler indicators that anger is building up. These might include changes in tone of voice, such as becoming more curt or sarcastic; alterations in body language, like clenching jaws or fists; or even withdrawal and silence, which can signify suppressed anger or resentment.

Psychological Underpinnings

The expression of anger is deeply tied to individual psychological processes, including stress response systems, coping mechanisms, and learned behaviors from past experiences. For instance, someone who grew up in an environment where anger was expressed through silence might resort to withdrawal as their primary mode of expressing anger.

Recognizing the warning signals of anger building up is crucial for controlling this powerful emotion and avoiding negative consequences.

Understanding these psychological factors is crucial for recognizing and addressing anger in a healthy manner.

Recognizing Subtle Signs

Awareness of the less obvious signs of anger requires a heightened sense of self-awareness and emotional intelligence. It involves paying attention to one's internal experiences and recognizing when cognitive distortions, such as overgeneralization or personalization, are amplifying the emotional response. This awareness can also extend to recognizing triggers in the environment or interactions with others that may subtly increase stress and, consequently, anger.

The Role of Physiology

Physiologically, anger activates the body's "fight or flight" response, leading to an increase in heart rate, blood pressure, and adrenaline levels. Recognizing these physiological changes can serve as an early warning system, signaling the need to employ coping strategies before anger escalates. Techniques such as deep breathing, mindfulness, or even physical activity can help regulate these physiological responses and prevent anger from manifesting in harmful behaviors.

Strategies for De-escalation

Effective management and de-escalation of anger involve both internal and external strategies. Internally, cognitive restructuring to challenge and change unhelpful thought patterns can reduce the intensity of anger. Externally, communication techniques that emphasize active listening, empathy, and assertiveness can help navigate situations that might otherwise lead to conflict. Recognizing the importance of context—understanding when and why certain behaviors appear—can aid in choosing the most appropriate strategy for de-escalation.

Expressions in Speech

Nonverbal clues such as speech patterns may also give light on how rage develops. Verbal manifestations of growing wrath include raising one's voice, using foul language, sarcasm, or threats. When uncontrolled, these emotions may heighten arguments and strain relationships. Individuals may encourage productive discourse and defuse potentially explosive circumstances by keeping an eye on their verbal communication and employing aggressive, non-confrontational language.

Physical Symptoms

Headaches, vertigo, nausea, or exhaustion are some of the physical symptoms that might accompany escalating rage. These outward signs mirror the physiological response to rage and, if untreated, may amplify emotional suffering. People may manage their physical symptoms and control their anger by exercising, using relaxation methods, or deep breathing exercises.

Being aware of the warning signals of anger escalation allows people to take preventative measures and develop healthy coping mechanisms. Anger may be better managed and health can be improved when people learn to be more self-aware and control their emotions. Recognizing and managing growing anger is crucial for sustaining good relationships and emotional well-being. This may be achieved by mindfulness practices, forceful communication, or relaxation methods.

Self-Assessment Quizzes

Quiz 1: Anger Level Evaluation Spielberger, C.D. (1999)

Instructions

Rate the following statements on a scale of 1 to 5, where 1 indicates strongly disagree and 5 indicates strongly agree.

✓ I often feel irritable or easily frustrated.

✓ My heart races and my breathing becomes shallow when I'm angry.

✓ I frequently experience muscle tension or clenched fists when angry.

✓ I have difficulty controlling my temper when things don't go my way.

✓ I often regret my actions or words during moments of anger.

✓ I find it challenging to calm down once I've become angry.

✓ Others have commented on my frequent displays of anger.

✓ I tend to hold grudges or dwell on past conflicts.

✓ I feel overwhelmed by my anger and struggle to manage it effectively.

✓ Anger interferes with my relationships and daily functioning.

Scoring

Add up your scores for each question to determine your overall anger level.

o 10-20: Low anger level

o 21-30: Moderate anger level

o 31-40: High anger level

o 41-50: Very high anger level

Quiz 2: Anger Trigger Identification

Instructions

Consider the following situations and indicate whether they trigger anger for you by selecting Yes or No.

✓ Being criticized or receiving negative feedback.

✓ Feeling disrespected or treated unfairly.

✓ Facing unexpected obstacles or setbacks.

✓ Dealing with uncooperative or incompetent individuals.

✓ Experiencing financial difficulties or stress.

✓ Interacting with family members during tense situations.

✓ Encountering traffic jams or delays during your commute.

✓ Witnessing acts of injustice or discrimination.

✓ Feeling overwhelmed by work or academic pressures.

✓ Experiencing physical discomfort or pain.

Scoring

Count the number of "Yes" responses to identify your primary anger triggers.

Key takeaways

- The sympathetic nervous system is activated and stress hormones are released as a result of anger, among other physiological reactions.
- Frustration, bitterness, and aggressiveness are just a few of the many emotions that may impact and be affected by anger. Anger may quickly spin out of control if people don't know to recognize the warning signals, such tense muscles and a racing heart.
- Anger management tools like self-assessment quizzes may help people figure out what makes them angry and how to control it.

Summary of actionable steps

- To control the physical reactions that anger causes, try mindfulness practices like deep breathing and progressive muscle relaxation.
- Discover the pain or fear that lies behind your rage and figure out how to deal with those emotions in a healthy way.
- To track changes in anger levels and evaluate success in anger management, take self-assessment quizzes on a regular basis.

- Regularly engaging in self-assessment quizzes can be instrumental in promoting effective anger management and emotional well-being. By reflecting on questions related to anger triggers, emotional responses, and coping strategies, individuals can cultivate increased self-awareness and identify recurring patterns in their anger experiences.
- Over time, this process allows individuals to track their progress, recognize areas for growth, and develop strategies for more adaptive emotional regulation.
- If you or someone you care about is having trouble controlling your anger, it's a brave move to reach out for support from those you trust, whether that's friends, family, or mental health experts.

In the next chapter, we explore the complex dynamics of relationships as we continue our trip across the landscape of fury. A strong emotion like anger may have a significant impact on our relationships with those closest to us, altering the very essence of our social bonds.

Understanding the nuances of conflict resolution, emotional expression, and communication becomes clearer as we delve into the ways anger plays out in different types of relationships in the next chapter. Gaining insight into the function of anger in relationships is critical for building strong connections and enduring partnerships, whether it's resolving conflicts with loved ones or dealing with societal disappointments. In Chapter 4, you will delve into the complex web of human connections and the powerful impact that anger can have on them.

CHAPTER 4

Anger in Relationships: Friends, Family, and Others

> *Emotions are contagious. We've all known it experientially.*
>
> – Daniel Goleman

IN EXPLORING THE dynamics of anger within relationships, it's crucial to acknowledge its profound impact on both individuals and the bonds they share. As renowned psychologist Daniel Goleman once remarked, "Emotions are contagious. We've all known it experientially." This sentiment underscores the profound influence of anger within interpersonal connections, where its effects can ripple far beyond the initial trigger. The quote suggests that while physical wounds may heal with time, the emotional scars left by anger often linger, sometimes indefinitely. By delving into the complexities of anger within various relationship contexts—be it with friends, family members, or acquaintances—we can gain a deeper understanding of its potential to fracture bonds, erode trust, and sow seeds of resentment. Thus, as we navigate the intricacies of anger within our social circles, it

> Understanding anger's impact on relationships underscores the importance of cultivating self-awareness, empathy, and effective communication for healthier interactions.

becomes imperative to cultivate self-awareness, empathy, and effective communication skills to foster healthier, more harmonious relationships.

Imagine that there is a rainstorm forming over the horizon. The dark clouds are whirling around with power, and they are about to let loose a flood of rain and lightning. Anger, like a storm, can be cruel and unpredictable, casting a shadow over our relationships and leaving wounds that are hard to heal. When you're among angry people, whether it's in your family, friends, or circle of acquaintances, have you ever been swept up in the waves? Anger can have a devastating effect on every connection, from the delicate dynamics of a strained friendship to the violent confrontations within family dynamics.

This chapter will take you on a trip into the complex web of relationships by examining the ways anger shows up and the damage it can do to our relationships. We will explore the hidden facts of rage in our closest relationships and learn ways for resolving disagreements with empathy and grace via an examination of tales, data, and questions designed to stimulate thinking.

Let us, therefore, prepare to face the waves of interpersonal dynamics head-on so that we may come out on the other side with a better grasp of what it takes to build stronger, healthier bonds with one another.

Navigating Anger in Friendships

While arguments and squabbles are part of each relationship, it may be difficult to manage anger in friendships. Having good and happy friendships depends on learning to balance your emotions. Learn all the ins and outs of handling rage in your friendships with this detailed guide:

Gaining Insight into Anger Dynamics

Trust, mutual respect, and shared experiences are the cornerstones of a strong friendship. On the other hand, disagreements could emerge when people's expectations aren't satisfied, boundaries are violated, or dialogue stops. Frustration, hurt, rage, and other negative emotions may arise from these disagreements and, if left unattended, can put a strain on the connection. The first step in overcoming arguments and building your connection is to identify what is really bothering you, such as unfulfilled wants or unfinished business.

> Navigating anger in friendships requires understanding underlying emotions, honest communication, and empathy to strengthen connections.

For instance, consider a scenario where a couple repeatedly argues about household chores. While the surface-level disagreement appears to revolve around the division of labor, deeper exploration may reveal that one partner feels undervalued and unappreciated for their contributions, while the other harbors resentment stemming from unvoiced expectations. Under such circumstances, the couple can shift their focus from assigning blame to collaboratively addressing core concerns through a simple candid discussion about their emotions and needs; thereby fostering understanding, empathy, and ultimately, a stronger connection.

Honest communication

The foundation of every healthy connection, including friendships, is open and honest communication. Use "I" sentences to explain your point of view without assigning blame; do it politely and gently. Inspire your buddy to open up about how they're feeling and thinking, and pay close attention so you can grasp their perspective. When people are able to communicate effectively, they are able to understand one another and share their thoughts and emotions without fear of repercussion.

Empathy is key

When dealing with rage in friendships, empathy is key. Validation is also important. Try to empathize with your buddy by placing yourself in their position. Acknowledge their experiences and show care and compassion to validate their sentiments. Express your willingness to be there for them and acknowledge that their sentiments are real. When people talk to one another with empathy, it makes everyone feel heard, appreciated, and supported.

Looking for a Solution

Resolving conflicts is crucial for dealing with anger in friendships and bringing peace again. Try to resolve the disagreement amicably with your friend's help. Come up with ideas for middle ground solutions that might satisfy both of your demands. Accept responsibility for your behavior and be ready to apologize if required. Finding common ground and deepening your relationship should take precedence over trying to "win" an issue. Resolve conflicts by showing empathy, being patient, and open to compromise.

Forgiveness

A key component of resolving anger in friendships is forgiving one another and moving on. Put your negative feelings towards your buddy in the past. Now is the time to move on. Keeping resentment and blame between friends only makes things worse. Rather, forgive one another and see the disagreement for what it really is: a chance to learn and develop. Make a pact to work on improving your relationship and accept the lessons you've learnt. Building a stronger, more resilient relationship is possible when you both practice forgiveness and embrace development. It will help you face obstacles together.

Finally, being able to communicate effectively, empathize, and being prepared to compromise are all necessary for friends to navigate anger. Your friendships will flourish and your relationships will be more supportive and understanding if you learn to control your anger, talk to each other honestly, establish healthy boundaries, and forgive yourself and others when you mess up.

Dealing with Anger in Family Settings

In family relationships, anger can often become entangled, resulting in heightened emotions and strained interactions. Understanding the unique dynamics at play within your family unit is essential for effectively managing anger and fostering healthier relationships. By recognizing the underlying patterns of communication, power structures, and emotional triggers within your family, you can gain valuable insights into why conflicts arise and how they can be addressed more constructively.

Acknowledging that it's normal to feel angry around relatives is the first step. Most people don't know you as well as your family does—or at least, not to the extent that you would like them to. While it's normal to be angry with your family, you must take full responsibility for how you act when you're angry

Taking responsibility for one's actions during moments of anger is crucial for fostering healthier relationships.

Be sure your expectations are reasonable

That is to say, you are inviting disappointment upon yourself if you think your family will act differently than they have shown you. Be honest with yourself and accept your family members for what they've shown you, flaws and all. You will have a greater chance of dealing with reality when you encounter it if you are prepared for it. Additionally, it will be simpler to avoid being furious with family members when they don't conform to your expectations if you can accept them as they are, flaws and all.

Acceptance of a family member doesn't necessitate full agreement with their views or behaviors; rather, it entails acknowledging and respecting their autonomy and inherent worth as individuals. This distinction allows for the cultivation of healthy boundaries and constructive communication within the family unit. For example, imagine a scenario where a parent holds political beliefs diametrically opposed to those of their adult child.

While the child may vehemently disagree with their parent's stance, they can still choose to honor their parent's autonomy and maintain a loving relationship by focusing on shared values, fostering open dialogue, and finding common ground where possible. By embracing the notion that acceptance doesn't equate to endorsement, family members can navigate differences with grace, empathy, and mutual respect, thereby preserving familial bonds while honoring their own convictions.

Take it easy on other people

Keep in mind that you are not obligated to share your views, behaviors, or interests with anybody else. You should be as understanding of other people's points of view as you would want to be treated with respect when you express your own. Another important thing to remember while dealing with rage around family is to be kind and tolerant of them, no matter how different they are from how you think they "should" be.

Rather than speaking to be understood, listen to understand

Listen with the intent to comprehend rather than just to be understood. The importance of listening to other people should not be underestimated, in my opinion. The more you make other people feel heard, the more probable it is that they will return the favor. Especially when it comes to members of one's own family. Put yourself in their shoes and listen to them without interjecting your own opinion. Your loved ones will appreciate it more. Like you probably want them to do for you, your chances of embracing someone for who they are improve the more you can see things from their point of view and comprehend their motivations.

Keep in mind that you are human and prone to

making errors

When you make a mistake, it's tempting to focus on yourself, but remember that your loved ones are also upset. We tend to focus on the pain that other people inflict on us and downplay the pain that we create on other people. Now that you know that, however, I believe it is your duty to take stock and acknowledge that you have harmed your family in many ways, whether purposefully or unintentionally. You may approach the relatives who are now upsetting you with greater humility after you have a better understanding of your own shortcomings.

Be kind while you lead.

While leading with kindness and compassion is often beneficial in resolving family disagreements, it's important to acknowledge the limitations of this approach, especially in situations where familial relationships are marked by toxicity or abuse. The sentiment that 'family is family' may not adequately address the depth of pain and trauma experienced by individuals who face ridicule, disownment, or other forms of mistreatment from family members.

In such cases, prioritizing one's own well-being, setting boundaries, and seeking support from trusted sources are essential steps in navigating challenging family dynamics. Encouraging dialogue about the complexities of familial relationships and promoting understanding while also acknowledging the need for accountability and self-protection can foster healthier relationships within families. Ultimately, genuine healing and reconciliation within family dynamics require empathy, understanding, and a commitment to addressing harmful behaviors and dynamics.

The Family Conflict

Imagine a married couple named Karen and Tom who have a history of heated arguments about money. These arguments eventually escalate and cause tension in their relationship with their children. Their incapacity to settle their financial differences has a negative impact on their family's trust and closeness, leading to a vicious circle of animosity and strife.

In this analysis, we see how the tensions between Tom and Karen show how lingering problems may affect family relationships. The stability and unity of their family unit are undermined by their chronic incapacity to communicate clearly and reach a consensus on money issues. Karen and Tom may fix their relationship and their family's financial situation by seeing a professional for help with their communication and relationship difficulties. This might be in the form of couples therapy or financial planning.

Important points: The most important thing to remember is that the best approach to fix family problems and build relationships is to talk things out, listen carefully, and work together to find solutions. Fostering a helpful and harmonious home environment is possible when families prioritize mutual respect and understanding. This allows them to persevere through financial difficulties and other stresses as a unit.

Healthy Boundary Setting

Navigating family relationships, particularly in the face of disagreement or conflict, requires a nuanced understanding of boundaries. Boundaries are the emotional, physical, and psychological limits that individuals establish to protect their well-being and maintain healthy relationships. They serve as guidelines for acceptable behavior and help delineate where one person ends and another begins within the context of relationships.

Establishing and enforcing boundaries in family relationships is essential for maintaining emotional well-being and fostering healthy connections.

Establishing boundaries involves identifying personal needs, values, and limits, as well as communicating them clearly and assertively to others. Boundaries can take various forms, such as:

Emotional boundaries: These involve respecting one's feelings, opinions, and autonomy. For example, setting limits on how much emotional support or involvement one is willing to provide in certain situations.

Physical boundaries: These relate to personal space and physical touch. They may include setting boundaries around personal belongings, personal space, or physical affection.

Time boundaries: These involve prioritizing one's time and energy and setting limits on how much time is allocated to specific activities or relationships.

Communication boundaries: These encompass how individuals communicate with each other and may involve setting guidelines for respectful communication, listening without judgment, and expressing needs and concerns assertively.

Implementing boundaries requires consistency, self-awareness, and assertiveness. It often involves practicing self-care, recognizing when boundaries are being violated, and taking steps to enforce them. This may include communicating boundaries directly and respectfully, seeking support from trusted friends or professionals, or limiting contact with individuals who repeatedly disregard boundaries.

Just as painting lines in the sand delineates where one person's rights stop and another's begin in the intricate dance of human interactions, defining limits does the same. Respectful relationships with others and our own emotional health depend on our ability to set and stick to appropriate boundaries when dealing with anger.

Adhering to Individual Boundaries

Boundaries are like a wall that keeps our mental, emotional, and bodily health protected. A foundation for acceptable and unacceptable conduct and treatment may be laid out by stating and conveying one's own boundaries. When we are self-aware, we can see when someone has crossed our limits and decide what to do about it.

Avoiding Hatred and Exhaustion

We risk being overwhelmed, angry, or worn out by other people's demands and expectations if we don't set clear limits for ourselves. In order to prevent burnout and resentment, it is important to establish appropriate limits that allow for time for self-care, relaxing, and recharging. By establishing clear limits, we may better organize our time and energy so that it serves our most important goals and fulfills our most pressing obligations.

Fostering Respectful Interactions

Rather than constructing barriers or excluding people, setting boundaries is an opportunity to cultivate relationships characterized by understanding, empathy, and mutual respect. We show people how much we value ourselves and how much we expect to be treated with decency and respect when we express our limits in a confident and polite way. By doing the same, we show that we value other people's independence and the ability to choose for themselves how we live our lives.

Case Studies and Analysis

Understanding the nuances of anger management in different social contexts is greatly enhanced by examining real-life examples. We may learn a lot about how to handle comparable situations in our own lives by looking at these examples and trying to understand the dynamics at work. As an example, let's look at a few case studies and analyze the main points:

1. The Conflict Between Siblings

Imagine this: Sarah and David are two siblings in their early teens who have a history of bickering about who gets what around the home.

Arguments and wounded emotions ensue as Sarah becomes bitter when David does not provide his fair part.

A failure to establish firm limits and communicate expectations on domestic duties is at the heart of this situation, according to the analysis. It's possible that David doesn't realize how his behaviors affect his sister, Sarah, who is frustrated because she feels overworked and undervalued. Sarah and David may develop clear limits and work out a fair distribution of responsibilities by listening to each other out and talking about what they anticipate. This will help them work together more effectively and reduce conflict.

Important Points: In order to resolve disagreements and encourage collaboration in sibling relationships, it is crucial to have effective communication, mutual respect, and well established limits. Stronger, more harmonious relationships based on understanding and empathy may be achieved when siblings confront underlying difficulties and negotiate compromises.

2. The Workplace Explosion

Imagine this: a team meeting takes a turn for the worst when Mark, the project manager, snaps at a coworker who challenges his leadership choices. The team's morale takes a nosedive as communication and cooperation go by the wayside as a result of his tantrum.

The destructive effects of uncontrolled emotions on the job are shown by Mark's furious outburst. His inability to control his temper has a negative impact on his career and team morale and output. Creating a more pleasant and supportive work environment is possible for Mark if he takes the time to focus on what makes him angry and finds other methods to handle criticism constructively.

Important Points: Facing difficult interpersonal dynamics at work requires emotional intelligence, self-awareness, and the ability to handle stress effectively. Individuals may react to workplace disagreements with professionalism and calm by developing resilience and using constructive coping mechanisms. This, in turn, promotes trust and cooperation among their teams.

Case studies are a great way to learn about the ins and outs of anger management in relationships. An individual's ability to handle disagreements, promote communication, and grow healthy, satisfying relationships may be enhanced by studying these cases and drawing important lessons.

Key takeaways

- When it comes to dealing with anger in social situations, such as friendships and family, it's crucial to communicate well. It is possible to keep relationships civil and conflict-free by establishing reasonable limits.
- People may learn to control their emotions and keep situations from becoming worse if they are aware of the warning signals.
- Successfully negotiating interpersonal problems and controlling anger may be learned by analyzing real-life case studies.

Summary of actionable steps

- To promote understanding and lessen disputes, make an effort to listen actively and empathize with other people when you engage with them.
- Make your wants and expectations known in an honest and forceful way, and set firm limits.
- You may learn to control your emotions by practicing mindfulness or relaxation methods and by learning to notice the bodily sensations or changes in mood that indicate an impending outburst of rage.
- Thinking about how you would handle similar circumstances (as discussed in the book) in real life, might help you develop healthy coping mechanisms for dealing with disagreements and building rapport.

Building emotional intelligence is an important part of maintaining emotional health, and it's time to move on from our previous discussion about rage in relationships. To better understand and control our emotions, we will explore this topic in depth in the upcoming chapter.

We will discover realistic ways to improve emotional intelligence, self-awareness, and relationship wellness.

Join us in Chapter 5 as we delve into the intriguing world of emotional intelligence, paving the way for increased emotional resilience and satisfaction.

Make a Difference with Your Review
Unlock the Power of Generosity

"Money can't buy happiness, but giving it away can." - Freddie Mercury

Did you know that people who give without expectation live longer, happier lives and make more money? So if we've got a shot at that during our time together, darn it, I'm gonna try. To make that happen, I have a question for you...

Who is this person, you ask? They're much like you. Or, at least, they're reminiscent of who you once were—less experienced, eager to make a difference, and seeking guidance but unsure where to find it.

Our **MISSION** is to make the wisdom of anger management accessible to everyone. Everything we do stems from that mission. And the only way for us to achieve that mission is by reaching... well... everyone.

This is where **YOU** come in. As much as we might wish otherwise, most people do judge a book by its cover (and its reviews). So here's my request on behalf of a struggling teen like the one you once were:

 Please lend your
VOICE to this book by **leaving a review.**

Your **CONTRIBUTION** requires **NO money** and takes less than 60 seconds, but it could change the **LIFE** of a fellow adolescent forever. Your **REVIEW** could help...
...another struggling teen find solace and support.
...a parent or caregiver understand and connect with their child better.
...a teacher or counselor provide more effective guidance to their students.
...a community foster empathy and understanding among its members.

To experience the satisfaction of making a real difference and aiding someone in need, all you have to do is... and it takes less than a minute... **LEAVE A REVIEW.**

Simply scan the QR code below to leave your review:

If you believe in the **POWER of EMPATHY** and support, you are my kind of person. **WELCOME** to the **CLUB.** **YOU'RE** one of **US.**

I'm even more thrilled to assist you in navigating the storms of adolescence and mastering your emotions than you can imagine. You'll find immense value in the strategies and insights I'm about to share in the **UPCOMING** chapters.

 THANK YOU from the depths of my heart. Now, let's get back to our journey of growth and understanding.

Your ally in the voyage, **Emma Davis**

 PS - Did you know? By providing value to others, you become more valuable to them. If you believe this book could benefit someone else, why not pass it along?

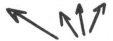

CHAPTER 5

Building Emotional Intelligence

The greatest ability in business is to get along with others and influence their actions

— John Hancock

HAVE YOU EVER pondered the reasons behind some people's seeming ease in handling life's obstacles and others' apparent difficulty with emotional regulation? There is a solution in emotional intelligence. "Emotional intelligence (EI), also known as emotional quotient (EQ), refers to the ability to recognize, understand, and manage one's own emotions, as well as to recognize, understand, and influence the emotions of others. It encompasses a range of skills and competencies that contribute to effective communication, empathy, self-awareness, and interpersonal relationships."

Here we'll go into why developing your emotional intelligence is so crucial, and how it may revolutionize your relationships at work and at home.

The exciting realm of emotional intelligence will be explored in this chapter, along with practical methods to increase it. What follows is a list of topics:

Understanding the importance of emotional intelligence (EI) is crucial for navigating life's challenges and fostering meaningful relationships.

- Grasping the concept of compassion and empathy handling
- Anticipations and dissatisfactions
- Improving one's self-consciousness and self-regulation
- Adventures in interactive storytelling and role-playing

Managing Expectations and Frustrations

> Learning to manage frustrations is not about erasing challenges but mastering how we respond to them, shaping our experiences and outcomes

The ability to empathize with another person's feelings and experiences is fundamental to developing genuine relationships with them. We show our readiness to grasp another person's point of view, validate their experiences, and recognize their emotions when we empathize with them. Fostering empathy reciprocity, establishing trust, and enabling open communication are all crucial aspects of anger management that rely on empathy.

Enhancing emotional intelligence

Emotional intelligence is a set of skills that helps us deal with difficult social situations, read body language, and keep our emotions in check. One of these skills is empathy. A more compassionate, understanding, and empathetic response to rage is possible when we train ourselves to be more in tune with our own and other people's feelings.

Empathy as conflict resolution tool

Empathy allows us to de-escalate tensions, diffuse animosity, and encourage reconciliation when we find ourselves in conflict situations. Understanding one another's feelings and points of view helps us establish areas of agreement, clear up confusion, and settle conflicts in a way that everyone is happy with. Being empathetic also helps us get to the bottom of things, which is crucial for fixing relationships and resolving conflicts in the long run.

The Role of Compassion in Promoting Health and Well-being

A compassionate person goes above and beyond mere empathy to motivate others to take action and help those in pain. Instead of retribution and blaming, we put an emphasis on understanding, forgiveness, and reconciliation when we handle anger compassionately. We foster an atmosphere conducive to recovery, development, and change when we show compassion to one another and to ourselves.

Promoting Atonement and Peace

When we practice compassion, we are able to let go of anger, forgive, and go on with our lives. Release yourself from the weight of bitterness and resentment by seeing the humanity and value in the people who have wronged you. This will help you heal and move on from broken relationships.

Emotional Health

Being compassionate helps people feel more connected to others and their common humanity, which in turn boosts their emotional health and resilience. We can all do our part to heal as a society and improve our social bonds by practicing self-compassion and then spreading that attitude to others around us.

Did You Know?

8% of people with moderate anger issues are likely to develop significant complications in their lives.

Dealing with Frustrations

Using Strategies for Dealing with Stress

- Reduce irritation and improve your mental health by making stress management a regular part of your life. Physical exercise, gradual muscular relaxation, deep breathing techniques, and mindfulness meditation are all examples of what can fall under this category.
- Try writing in a diary, creating art, or engaging in a relaxing hobby as healthy ways to release pent-up irritation. Rather of letting feelings linger and worsen, it might be helpful to express them in productive ways.

Trying to Find Help

- When you're struggling with intense anger, don't be afraid to ask for help from someone you trust, whether that's loved ones or mental health experts. When times are tough, it helps to talk to someone you trust for an outside viewpoint, affirmation, and advise.
- If stress and frustration are getting the best of you, it may be time to join a support group or consult a therapist. More efficient navigation of challenging emotions may be facilitated by the specific tactics and coping skills offered by a qualified therapist.

You may improve your health, emotional intelligence, and resilience by learning to manage your expectations and frustrations in a healthy way. Frustration is a natural human emotion, but how you deal with it determines the quality of your experience and the results you get.

Developing Self-awareness and Self-control

Enhancing self-awareness and self-control involves a multifaceted approach aimed at deepening our understanding of ourselves and refining our ability to regulate our emotions. Here's a breakdown of key aspects to consider:

Mindfulness Practices

Engage in mindfulness meditation: Regular meditation practice can help cultivate present-moment awareness, allowing you to observe your thoughts, emotions, and bodily sensations without judgment.

Practice mindful breathing: Focus on your breath as it moves in and out of your body, using it as an anchor to bring your attention back to the present moment whenever you feel overwhelmed by anger.

Incorporate mindfulness into daily activities: Bring mindfulness to everyday tasks such as eating, walking, or washing dishes, by paying attention to the sensations, thoughts, and emotions that arise.

Reflection Exercises

Self-inquiry: Ask yourself probing questions to deepen your self-awareness, such as "What situations or interactions tend to trigger my anger?" or "How do I typically respond when I feel angry?"

Practical Strategies

Recognize early warning signs: Learn to identify the physical, emotional, and behavioral cues that signal escalating anger, such as increased heart rate, tension in the body, or negative thought patterns.

Pause and breathe: When you notice these warning signs, take a moment to pause and take several deep breaths. This simple act can help interrupt the automatic stress response and provide a brief window of opportunity to choose a more constructive response.

Use relaxation techniques: Practice relaxation techniques such as progressive muscle relaxation or guided imagery to help release tension and promote a sense of calmness.

Develop coping strategies: Explore healthy coping mechanisms to manage anger, such as exercise, creative expression, or talking to a trusted friend or therapist.

Reframe negative thoughts: Challenge and reframe irrational or distorted thoughts that fuel anger, replacing them with more balanced and realistic perspectives.

> "Self-awareness and self-control are the twin pillars upon which personal growth and emotional resilience are built, empowering us to navigate life's challenges with clarity and composure."

Set boundaries: Establish clear boundaries in your relationships and communicate them assertively to others. Boundaries help protect your emotional well-being and prevent situations that may trigger anger.

By incorporating these practices and strategies into your daily life, you can gradually enhance your self-awareness and self-control, empowering yourself to navigate anger more effectively and cultivate greater emotional intelligence.

Interactive Stories and Role-Playing Scenarios

Utilizing interactive stories and role-playing scenarios can be a dynamic and engaging way to deepen understanding and practice skills related to emotional intelligence and anger management. Here's how these approaches can be implemented effectively:

Interactive Stories

- Craft narratives that depict characters facing situations involving anger and emotional challenges.
- Incorporate relatable characters and realistic scenarios that resonate with the audience's experiences.
- Introduce various outcomes and consequences based on the characters' choices and actions, highlighting the impact of different responses to anger.
- Encourage readers or participants to actively engage with the story by reflecting on the characters' emotions, motivations, and decision-making processes.
- Facilitate group discussions or individual reflections following the story to explore key themes, lessons learned, and potential strategies for managing anger.

Role-Playing Scenarios

- Design role-playing scenarios that simulate real-life interpersonal interactions and conflict situations.
- Assign roles to participants and provide them with specific instructions and objectives based on the scenario.
- Encourage participants to embody their assigned roles authentically, expressing thoughts, emotions, and behaviors consistent with their character.
- Facilitate the role-play exercise by providing guidance, feedback, and prompts as needed to support constructive engagement and learning.
- After the role-play, debrief the experience with participants, inviting reflections on the dynamics of the interaction, the effectiveness of different communication styles, and strategies for managing anger in similar situations.

Benefits and Learning Outcomes

Participants can glean valuable insights and learning from interactive stories and role-playing scenarios by actively engaging with the content and reflecting on their own experiences and behaviors.

"Engaging in interactive stories and role-playing scenarios offers a dynamic pathway to deepen emotional intelligence and cultivate effective anger management skills. Through relatable narratives and authentic simulations, participants can explore diverse perspectives, practice decision-making, and foster empathy, ultimately enhancing self-awareness and interpersonal relationships."

Participants can relate to the characters in the stories or scenarios by recognizing similar emotions, situations, or challenges they have faced in their own lives. By empathizing with the characters' experiences, participants can gain a deeper understanding of the complexities of anger and emotional challenges.

Interactive stories often present characters with choices and depict the consequences of those choices. Participants can reflect on the outcomes of different decisions made by the characters and consider how these outcomes relate to their own decision-making processes in real life. This exploration encourages self-reflection and awareness of the impact of one's actions on oneself and others.

Enhances empathy and perspective-taking: Interactive stories and role-playing allow participants to step into the shoes of others, fostering empathy and understanding of diverse perspectives.

Promotes experiential learning: By actively participating in simulated scenarios, individuals can practice applying emotional intelligence skills in a safe and supportive environment, reinforcing learning through experience.

82

Encourages problem-solving and decision-making: Engagement in interactive stories and role-playing prompts individuals to think critically, make informed choices, and consider the consequences of their actions, enhancing their ability to navigate real-life challenges effectively.

Facilitates skill transfer: Participants can transfer insights gained from interactive storytelling and role-playing exercises to their daily interactions and relationships, improving their capacity to manage anger and communicate assertively.

Incorporating interactive stories and role-playing scenarios into educational or therapeutic settings provides a dynamic platform for exploring complex emotional issues, building essential skills, and promoting personal growth and development.

Key Takeaways

- Understanding empathy and compassion is crucial for managing anger effectively, as it allows individuals to connect with others' emotions and perspectives.
- Managing expectations involves setting realistic goals and learning to adapt to unforeseen challenges, reducing the likelihood of frustration and anger.
- Developing self-awareness and self-control empowers individuals to recognize and regulate their emotions, leading to more constructive responses to anger-provoking situations.
- Interactive stories and role-playing scenarios offer immersive opportunities to practice emotional intelligence skills and explore effective strategies for managing anger.

Summary of Actionable Steps

- Practice active listening and empathy by genuinely seeking to understand others' feelings and perspectives during conflicts or disagreements.
- Set realistic expectations for yourself and others, acknowledging limitations and potential obstacles while striving for achievable goals.
- Cultivate self-awareness through regular reflection and mindfulness practices, such as journaling or meditation, to identify triggers and patterns of anger.
- Develop self-control by implementing relaxation techniques, such as deep breathing or visualization, to calm the body and mind in moments of anger.
- Engage in interactive storytelling or role-playing exercises to hone emotional intelligence skills and experiment with different approaches to managing anger-inducing scenarios.

By incorporating these actionable steps into your daily life, you can enhance your emotional intelligence and cultivate healthier responses to anger, ultimately fostering more harmonious relationships and greater well-being.

After exploring the intricacies of building emotional intelligence in Chapter 5, it's time to delve deeper into coping mechanisms and techniques in Chapter 6. In this next chapter, we will uncover a plethora of strategies designed to help you navigate through challenging emotions, including anger, with grace and resilience. From mindfulness practices to cognitive-behavioral techniques, you'll discover a toolkit of resources to empower you in managing your emotional well-being. So, let's embark on this journey together and uncover the secrets to mastering the art of coping.

CHAPTER 6

Coping Mechanisms and Techniques

Between stimulus and response there is a space. In that space is our power to choose our response. In our response lies our growth and our freedom.

– Viktor E. Frankl

IMAGINE YOU'RE HOLDING a remote control that can pause, rewind, or fast-forward through your emotions at will. What if we told you that, while life doesn't come with a remote, you do possess the power to control your emotional responses? This chapter is your guide to unlocking that power.

In this journey through Chapter 6: Coping Mechanisms and Techniques, we'll explore three transformative skills:

- Look into techniques that can instantly switch your body from a state of stress to one of calm, and discover mindfulness practices that let you observe your emotions without being swept away by them.

> "Your intellect may be confused, but your emotions will never lie to you." - Roger Ebert

- Learn how to voice your thoughts and feelings in an assertive yet respectful way, turning potential conflicts into opportunities for understanding and connection.

- Gain strategies for recognizing when emotions are about to overflow and how taking a strategic pause can prevent a cascade of unwanted reactions.

By the end of this chapter, you'll be equipped with practical tools not just to manage your emotions but to navigate life's ups and downs with greater ease and confidence. And that is an incentive as good as it gets.

Breathing Exercises and Mindfulness

When anger hits, it feels like a storm brewing inside, doesn't it? Everything tenses up, your heart beats faster, and your thoughts might start racing. It's like being on a small boat in the middle of a tempest. But what if you had the power to calm the seas? That's where breathing exercises and mindfulness come into play. Let's break it down.

Chill-Out Breathing

First up, let's talk about taking a deep breath. Sounds simple, right? But when you're seeing red, breathing deeply is like hitting the pause button on a rage-filled movie scene. Here's how to do it:

Deep Breathing: This isn't your average "take a breath" advice. It's about breathing so deep that your belly feels like it's going to pop. Imagine a balloon filling up in your stomach. Inhale through your nose slowly, hold that breath for a sec, and then let it out through your mouth like you're blowing out candles on your birthday cake. Aim for about 4-6 breaths per minute. This isn't a race; it's about returning to your chill zone.

4-7-8 Technique: This one's like a magic spell for your body. Breathe in quietly through your nose for 4 seconds, hold that breath for 7 seconds, and then whoosh it all out through your mouth for 8 seconds. It's a bit like hitting the reset button on your emotions.

Mindfulness: Your Secret Weapon

Now, for the mindfulness part. Mindfulness might sound a bit out there, like something only people who climb mountains and meditate for hours do. But it's actually super simple and super powerful, especially when you're about to lose it.

Be in the Now: Next time you're fuming, pause and notice five things around you. It could be the sound of a fan, the color of the sky, how your feet feel on the ground – anything. This brings you back to the present, away from whatever's winding you up.

Emotion Detective: Become a detective of your own emotions. When you're angry, ask yourself, "What's really bugging me?" Is it that comment someone made, or is it really about being tired or stressed? Figuring this out can be like finding the off switch for your anger.

> Mindfulness serves as a potent antidote to anger, offering simple yet effective techniques like focusing on the present moment and observing one's breath to regain composure and inner peace.

Mindful Breathing: Combine the first two by focusing all your attention on your breath. Feel it coming in, filling you with calm, and then going out, taking a bit of the anger with it. It's like you're breathing in peace and breathing out the storm.

And there you have it. Next time you're on the brink of a meltdown, remember these tricks. Deep breaths, a dash of mindfulness, and you've got this. It's about taking control back when your emotions are doing their best to run wild. Give it a shot, and you'll see how these simple tweaks can make a massive difference.

Did You Know?

An estimated 30% of people seek professional help due to anger-related problems.

Assertive Communication

Alright, let's dive into the art of talking it out without blowing up or shutting down. You know those moments when you're so ticked off you either want to scream or go silent? There's actually a sweet spot between those two, and it's called being assertive. Let's break down how to get your point across without starting World War III or becoming a doormat.

Finding Your Assertive Sweet Spot

I Statements: This is your golden ticket. Instead of saying "You make me so mad!" try "I feel upset when this happens." It's like saying, "Hey, this is about me and my feelings, not about blaming you." It takes the heat off the other person and makes it way easier to have a real conversation.

Listen Up: Good talkers are also great listeners. Even if you think you know what the other person is going to say, give them the floor. Listening isn't just about waiting for your turn to speak; it's about really hearing them out. Sometimes, just feeling heard can dial down the tension big time.

Keep Your Cool: Easier said than done, right? But here's the thing: the moment you lose your temper, your message gets lost in translation. If you need to, take a few of those deep breaths we talked about before jumping into the conversation. Staying calm shows you're in control and makes the other person more likely to listen.

Agree to Disagree: Sometimes, you're just not going to see eye to eye, and that's okay. You can respectfully agree to disagree. It's like saying, "I get where you're coming from, but here's my perspective." This can actually strengthen relationships because it's built on mutual respect.

Practice Makes Perfect: These skills might feel a bit awkward at first, like trying on a new pair of shoes. But the more you practice, the more natural it'll feel. Start with small stuff, and gradually, you'll become a pro at handling the big issues without losing your cool or your voice.

Real-Life Application

Let's say your friend keeps bailing on plans last minute, and it's driving you up the wall. Instead of blowing up at them, you could say, "I feel really disappointed when our plans fall through. It makes me feel like our time together isn't important to you." Then, give them a chance to explain. Maybe they're going through something you didn't know about. From there, you can work on a solution together, like making plans that are easier to stick to.

Becoming assertive is like learning a new language—the language of respecting yourself and others. It's about getting your point across without crossing the line. And the cool part? It actually leads to deeper connections with the people around you because you're coming from a place of honesty and respect. So, give it a try. You might be surprised at how much smoother your conversations can go.

Time-Out Strategies for Immediate Relief

Ever felt like your emotions were a runaway train, and you're just along for the ride? One minute you're fine, and the next, you're about to blow a fuse. That's when you know you need a time-out, not the kind you got as a kid, but a grown-up version that actually helps you

cool down and come back stronger. Here's how to hit the pause button on those wild emotions before they take over.

Hit Pause with These Time-Out Tips

Recognize the Signs: The first step is knowing when you're about to lose it. Maybe your heart starts racing, or you feel the heat creeping up your neck. Or you may be feeling an urge to scream or yell. When you notice these signs, it's your cue to step back.

Say It Out Loud: If you're with someone and feel yourself getting heated, it's totally okay to say, "Hey, I need a minute to cool down." This isn't running away from the problem; it's making sure you don't say something you'll regret.

Find Your Chill Zone: Figure out what calms you down. Is it listening to music? Taking a walk? Sketching? Whatever it is, go do that. The point is to give your brain a break from whatever's winding you up.

Set a Timer: Give yourself a set amount of chill time. Maybe start with 10 minutes. During this time, do your best not to think about what made you mad. It's like giving your emotions a timeout so when you come back, you're not as emotionally charged.

Breathing Break: Never underestimate the power of breathing. Try the 4-7-8 technique we discussed, or take deep breaths. It's like hitting the reset button on your body's natural stress response.

Reflect, Don't Ruminate: There's a fine line between thinking over what happened and obsessing over it. Use your time-out to think about how you want to respond, not to stew in your anger. It's about finding a solution, not fueling the fire.

Putting It into Practice

Let's say you're in the middle of a heated argument with a friend, and you feel that anger bubbling up. Instead of letting it boil over, you say, "I need a few minutes to cool off." You step outside, take a walk, and focus on your breathing. As you walk, you start to think about why you're so upset and how you can explain your feelings without blaming or yelling.

When you come back, you're calmer and ready to have a more productive conversation. You've not only saved the situation from worsening but also shown yourself and your friend that you're committed to handling conflicts maturely.

Remember, taking a time-out isn't a sign of weakness; it's a strategy of strength. It shows you're in control of your emotions, not the other way around. So next time you feel that emotional tide rising, know that it's okay to take a step back and regroup. Your future self (and probably everyone around you) will thank you.

Step-by-Step Guides and Exercises

Alright, let's make this as practical as jeans with extra pockets. Here's a hands-on guide to master those techniques we just talked about, so you can keep your cool and communicate like a pro. Ready to dive in? Let's go!

6.4 Step-by-Step Guides and Exercises
Breathing Exercises & Mindfulness Practice

Exercise 1: The 4-7-8 Breathing Drill

Step 1: Find a quiet spot. Sit or lie down comfortably.

Step 2: Close your eyes, and take a normal breath.

Step 3: Now, inhale quietly through your nose for 4 seconds.

Step 4: Hold that breath for 7 seconds.

Step 5: Exhale completely through your mouth, making a whoosh sound, for 8 seconds.

Step 6: Repeat this cycle four times.

Why This Works: It's like a chill pill for your nervous system, helping you reset and calm down fast.

Exercise 2: Mindful Observation

Step 1: Pick an object nearby (a plant, a cup, a pencil).

Step 2: Spend the next few minutes examining it. Notice its colors, textures, and how the light hits it.

Step 3: If your mind wanders, gently bring your attention back to the object.

Why This Works: It trains your brain to focus on the present, cutting through the noise of your emotions.

Effective Communication Skills

Exercise 1: The "I Feel" Script

Step 1: Think of a recent situation where you felt misunderstood or upset.

Step 2: Write down what happened, focusing on your feelings. Use "I feel [emotion] when [situation] because [reason]."

Step 3: Share this script with a friend or family member, or practice saying it out loud to yourself.

Why This Works: It helps you articulate your feelings clearly without placing blame, paving the way for healthier conversations.

Exercise 2: Active Listening Role Play

Step 1: Pair up with a friend or family member.

Step 2: Take turns sharing a story or talking about your day for 3 minutes.

Step 3: The listener should focus entirely on the speaker, nodding and responding with relevant questions or comments.

Step 4: After each turn, discuss how it felt to be heard and to listen.

Why This Works: It sharpens your listening skills, a crucial part of effective communication.

Time-Out Strategies for Immediate Relief

Exercise 1: Personal Pause Button

Step 1: Create a list of signs that show you're getting heated (clenched fists, fast heartbeat).

Step 2: Decide on a 'pause button' action (deep breathing, counting to 10, stepping outside).

Step 3: Next time you notice those signs, hit your pause button.

Why This Works: It gives you a direct way to interrupt escalating emotions, giving you space to cool off.

Exercise 2: Emotion Journaling

Step 1: Keep a small notebook with you.

Step 2: Whenever you take a time-out, write down what triggered you, how you felt, and how you responded.

Step 3: Reflect on these entries once a week to see patterns and progress.

Why This Works: It increases your self-awareness, helping you better understand and manage your triggers.

Bringing It All Together

These exercises aren't just tasks; they're tools in your emotional toolkit. Like any skill, the more you practice, the better you get. So, don't stress if it feels awkward at first. Keep at it, and soon, you'll find yourself handling emotions and conversations with much more confidence and less stress. Let's get practicing!

Key Takeaways of the Chapter

- Breathing exercises and mindfulness can dramatically lower stress and help manage anger.
- Effective communication involves expressing your feelings assertively, not aggressively, using "I" statements.
- Taking a time-out when emotions run high allows you to respond rather than react.
- Practicing these techniques regularly can improve your emotional intelligence and relationships.

Summary of Actionable Steps

- Practice the 4-7-8 technique daily to reset your stress response.
- Spend 5 minutes observing an object to ground yourself in the present.
- Write and practice expressing your feelings without blaming others.
- Engage in a role-play to enhance your listening skills.
- Identify your emotional triggers and decide on a pause button action.
- Keep track of your triggers and responses to increase self-awareness.

Ready to level up your emotional intelligence game? In the next chapter, we're going deeper into the world of emotions. Ever wonder why certain things tick you off or make you super happy? We're going to uncover the mysteries of our emotional triggers, learn how to set personal boundaries, and explore how understanding others' emotions can enrich our lives.

Don't miss out on mastering your emotional universe. It's time to turn the page and discover the keys to coping with your emotions and thriving.

CHAPTER 7

Transforming Anger into Positive Energy

For every minute you remain angry, you give up sixty seconds of peace of mind.

– Ralph Waldo Emerson

HOLDING ONTO ANGER is like grasping a hot coal with the intent of throwing it at someone else. The outcome: you are the only one who gets burned. This simple wisdom reminds us that anger, while a natural emotion, can cause more harm to ourselves than to the target of our frustrations. But what if we could transform that intense energy into something positive, something life-changing?

> Transforming anger into positive energy involves harnessing its intense force and redirecting it towards growth and Fulfillment.

In this chapter, we're embarking on a transformative journey, turning the fiery force of anger into a beacon of creativity, connection, and growth. We'll explore how channeling your anger into creative and passionate pursuits can not only diffuse negative emotions but also ignite a spark of innovation and joy in your life. We'll dive into the rewarding world of volunteering and community engagement, showing you how lending a hand can shift your focus and provide a profound sense of purpose and fulfillment. Finally, we'll tackle personal development projects, guiding you through setting and achieving goals that manage your anger and contribute to your personal and professional growth. Get ready to turn the heat of your anger into the light of positive change.

Did You Know?

Stoic philosophy is known for teaching self-awareness and self-control. The next time you get angry over someone else's actions, think of the great stoic philospher Marcus Aurelius, who said: "The best revenge is to be unlike him who performed the injury."

---

0 Creativity and Passion

Ever noticed how some of the most intense, passionate art or groundbreaking projects come from a place of deep emotion? That's because emotions like anger aren't just roadblocks; they can be rocket fuel for creativity. Instead of letting anger control you, channel it into something amazing. Here's how to make that shift.

Turn the Heat into a Beat

Artistic Expression: Ever heard of "anger art"? It's time to create some. Grab a canvas, some paint, clay, or even your old guitar, and pour all that intense energy into creating. Don't think about making it perfect; just let it out. You might just end up with something raw, real, and compelling.

Writing It Down: Angry? Good. Let's write. Start a journal, write a poem, or even a short story. Use your words to paint a picture of what you're feeling. This isn't just about venting; it's about transforming those fiery emotions into narratives that resonate and connect.

Passion Projects: Got a cause you're fired up about? Use that energy to fuel a project or campaign. Whether it's environmental activism, social justice, or anything else that gets your blood boiling, channeling your anger into action can lead to significant change and personal growth.

Physical Expression: Sometimes, you've just gotta move. Dance, run, do martial arts—anything that gets you into your body and out of your head. Physical activity can turn the adrenaline rush of anger into productive energy, leaving you calmer and more focused afterward.

Making the Shift: From Fury to Fuel

Acknowledge the Fire: First, recognize that feeling angry is okay, it's natural. Denying it only gives it more power. Acknowledge your anger; then decide to use it as a catalyst for something positive.

Choose Your Outlet: Experiment with different creative outlets to find what works best for you. It might be something you've never tried before, so be open to exploring.

Set a Routine: Make a habit of channeling your emotions into your chosen outlet. Regular practice not only helps manage anger but also improves your skills in that area, whether it's art, writing, or advocacy.

Reflect on the Process: After you've spent some time in your creative pursuit, take a step back and reflect. How did it make you feel? Did it help you see your anger in a different light? Often, the act of creation provides new perspectives on our emotions.

The Outcome

Channeling anger into creativity and passion doesn't just neutralize a negative emotion; it transforms it into something that can add meaning, purpose, and beauty to your life. It's about taking something that feels destructive and turning it into a force for creation. So next time you feel that familiar surge of anger, remember: within it lies potential energy, waiting to be unleashed in the most beautiful and impactful ways.

Physical Activity as an Anger Outlet

You know that feeling when you're so ticked off you could either scream into a pillow or run a marathon? Well, it turns out, choosing the marathon (or any physical activity) might just be one of the best decisions you can make for yourself. Let's dive into why working up a sweat is a fantastic way to work out your anger.

Let's explore why breaking a sweat can be a powerful strategy for dealing with anger.

The Science Bit

When you're angry, your body is in a heightened state of arousal; your heart rate goes up, your muscles tense, and your body gears up for action. This is all thanks to our buddy adrenaline. Back in the caveman days, this was super useful for the whole "fight or flight" thing. But in today's world, where the sources of our anger are less about survival and more about, say, frustrating group projects or traffic jams, throwing a punch or sprinting away isn't exactly the most socially acceptable response.

Why Physical Activity Rocks for Anger Management

While we may have evolved beyond our cave-dwelling ancestors, the need for adrenaline persists in our daily lives for optimal functioning. Nevertheless, it's crucial to provide outlets for the surge of energy and adrenaline triggered by anger. Engaging in physical activity offers an effective means to dissipate this energy in real-time, preventing its redirection towards negative outlets like slamming doors or getting into a fight. However, this is just one of the benefits worth exploring; there are more discussed below:

Burns Off Steam: Physical activity uses up the excess energy that anger produces. After a solid workout, you're likely to find that you've not only burned calories but also burned off much of that anger.

Mood Booster: Ever heard of endorphins? They're those feel-good hormones that are released when you exercise. They're nature's painkillers and mood lifters, capable of turning a frown upside down.

Distraction: Getting into a physical activity can take your mind off whatever's bugging you. It's hard to stew over an argument when you're focused on nailing a yoga pose or beating your personal best in the pool.

Perspective Shift: After a workout, you might just find that you're looking at the situation with fresh eyes. Maybe it's the endorphins talking or the physical distance from the problem, but things often seem more manageable post-exercise.

Getting Physical with Your Anger

Team Sports: Not only do you get to channel that anger into the game, but the social aspect can also boost your mood.

Running or Cycling: These are great for clearing your mind, plus you get to distance yourself from your stressors physically.

Yoga: It combines physical activity with mindfulness, helping you to calm both body and mind.

Boxing: Hitting a punching bag can be incredibly satisfying when you're angry, providing a direct outlet for that fiery energy.

Next time you feel your temper flaring, consider lacing up those sneakers or rolling out the yoga mat. Not only will you be doing something good for your body, but you'll also be taking a proactive step towards managing your anger in a healthy way. So, why not turn that rage into a more positive energy? Your mind (and perhaps your punching bag) will thank you for it.

Volunteering and Community Engagement

Imagine turning the heat of your anger into a warm glow that lights up someone else's life. Sounds pretty amazing, right? That's exactly what volunteering and getting involved in your community can do. Let's unpack why channeling your anger through acts of kindness and service is in the best interests of you and your community.

Anger can actually help us make the world a fairer place. When people get upset about unfair treatment because of race, this feeling can push them to do something good about it. There's a special kind of anger that's really important for fighting against racism. This isn't about being mean or getting back at someone; it's about wanting to make big changes so that everyone is treated fairly.

This helpful anger is focused on stopping racism and making sure everyone has the same chances and rights. It gets people talking and working together to fix what's wrong and to get rid of unfair rules and behaviors.

Sometimes, when people see or face racism, they get very angry in a way that makes them want to act. This is especially true for people who have to deal with unfairness in many parts of their lives, like people of color, women, or those who don't have a lot of money.

> Volunteering and community engagement offer avenues for channeling frustration into impactful actions.

Actions like protesting or speaking up at school or work are ways people use their anger in a good way. They're trying to make everyone aware of the problem and work together to fix it.

People who want to support others in fighting racism need to listen and help lift up the voices of those who are being treated unfairly. It's not helpful if they try to make it all about their own anger. They should use their anger to help make changes and not just to show off on the internet.

By understanding and using our anger in the right way, we can all help make things better. This means not just getting mad but doing something about it, like joining in protests or helping others understand why racism is a big problem that needs to be fixed

The Power of Giving Back

When you're boiling over with frustration or anger, it might feel counterintuitive to focus on helping others. But that's the beauty of it— giving back has a way of putting our troubles into perspective, melting away our anger and replacing it with something much more fulfilling. Volunteering works as an anger outlet in a multitude of ways.

Shifts Your Focus: It takes your mind off whatever's grinding your gears and redirects your energy towards something positive and productive.

Builds Connections: Anger can often make us feel isolated or misunderstood. Volunteering connects us with others, reminding us of the shared human experience and the kindness of strangers.

Boosts Self-Esteem: Knowing you've made a tangible difference in someone's life is an instant mood lifter. It's hard to stay mad when you're filled with a sense of purpose and accomplishment.

Teaches Gratitude: Engaging with those who may be less fortunate or facing their own struggles can foster a sense of gratitude for what we have, diluting feelings of anger and resentment.

How to Get Started

Find Your Cause: What are you passionate about? Animals, the environment, helping the homeless? There's a cause for everything.

Start Small: You don't have to dive into a huge commitment right away. Look for one-off opportunities like a community clean-up day or helping out at a local event.

Bring a Friend: Feeling nervous or unsure? Drag a friend along. It's more fun and less daunting when you're not alone.

Reflect: After volunteering, take a moment to reflect on the experience. How did it make you feel? Did you notice a shift in your mood or perspective?

Next time anger starts to bubble up inside you, consider stepping outside of your own headspace and into a role where you can make a difference. Whether it's tutoring kids, walking shelter dogs, or planting trees, your actions can light up dark places, both in your community and within yourself.

By volunteering, you're not just dispelling your own anger; you're also spreading positivity, and in today's world, that's something we could all use a little more of. So, why not transform your fiery energy into a force for good? Your heart, head, and maybe even a few new friends will thank you for it.

Personal Development Projects

Ever thought about channeling your anger into something that's just for you? Something that helps you cool down and leaves you with a new skill, a sense of achievement, or even a better understanding of who you are? Personal development projects are all about turning that inner turmoil into a stepping stone for growth. Let's dive into how you can make your anger work for you, not against you.

> Personal development projects offer a transformative outlet for channeling anger into self-improvement and growth.

Turning Anger Into Ambition

Anger, while often seen as negative, can be a powerful motivator. It signals that something's not right, pushing us towards change. By focusing on personal development projects, you transform that restless energy into something productive, something that builds rather than destroys.

Project Ideas to Get You Started

Learn Something New: Ever wanted to play the guitar, code, speak another language, or master the art of cooking? Now's your chance. Pick something that excites you, keeps you engaged, and provides a satisfying outlet for your energy.

Fitness Goals: Setting physical goals can be incredibly rewarding. Whether it's running a 5K, mastering a yoga pose, or simply committing to a daily walk, physical activity is a proven way to reduce anger and stress.

Creative Expressions: Channel your emotions into art. Painting, writing, dancing, or any form of creative expression can be therapeutic, helping to process and express feelings in a constructive way.

Mindfulness and Meditation: Building a practice of mindfulness or meditation can be a game-changer in managing anger. Start with just a few minutes a day, and explore different techniques to find what works best for you.

Volunteer Project: Create a personal volunteering project. Identify a need in your community and devise a plan to address it. This could be anything from starting a community garden to organizing a local clean-up.

How to Stay on Track

Set Clear Goals: Define what success looks like for your project. Having clear, achievable goals will help keep you motivated.

Track Your Progress: Keep a journal or log of your progress. Seeing how far you've come can be a huge boost on days when motivation is low.

Celebrate Milestones: Set milestones within your project and celebrate when you reach them. This keeps you motivated and helps you associate positive feelings with your efforts.

Reflect on the Journey: Regularly take time to reflect on how the project is impacting your anger management. Are you finding it easier to control your anger? Do you feel more fulfilled?

From Anger to Achievement

Personal development projects offer a unique way to harness the energy of your anger and direct it towards something positive. They're about more than just distraction; they're about transformation. By committing to personal growth, you're not only managing your anger; you're also building a richer, more satisfying life. So, what project will you start today?

Key Takeaways

- Anger can be a powerful catalyst for creativity and passion, leading you to explore and deepen your interests and talents.
- Physical activity is a highly effective outlet for releasing and managing anger, improving both your mental and physical health.
- Volunteering and community engagement not only helps channel anger positively but also connects you with others and fosters a sense of fulfillment.
- Personal development projects provide a constructive way to use anger for growth, learning, and self-improvement.

Summary of Actionable Steps

- Identify an activity or hobby that excites you and dedicate time to it each week.
- Set a physical fitness goal, whether it's a daily walk, joining a sports team, or practicing yoga, and track your progress.
- Find a local organization or cause you care about and commit to volunteering a certain number of hours per month.
- Choose a skill or area for personal development, outline specific goals, and create a timeline for achieving them.

As we close this chapter on transforming anger into positive energy, you've equipped yourself with powerful tools for turning feelings of frustration and anger into forces for good. But our journey doesn't end here.

In the next chapter, we will explore one of the most challenging yet rewarding aspects of personal growth. Learn how to release the weights of resentment and bitterness that may hold you back, and discover how forgiveness can open up new pathways to peace and happiness.

CHAPTER 8

Digital Age Anger Management

Technology is a useful servant but a dangerous master.

– Christian Lous Lange

I N AN AGE where our lives are intertwined with digital devices, scrolling through social media and battling inbox overload has become as routine as brushing our teeth. But what happens to our emotions, specifically our anger, in this always-connected world? This chapter delves into the digital roots of modern anger, offering insights and solutions for navigating the tumultuous waters of online interactions without capsizing your emotional well-being.

As our reliance on technology grows, so does the potential for digital platforms to amplify emotions, including anger.

We're breaking down the digital age dilemma, from the impact of digital media on our anger to crafting healthy digital habits, harnessing technology for anger management, and even taking on digital detox challenges. It's time to reclaim your peace of mind in the Information Age.

The Impact of Digital Media on Anger

Digital media consumption can swiftly trigger emotional responses

Navigating the digital landscape can feel like riding a rollercoaster with your emotions strapped in right beside you. One minute you're laughing at a cute cat video, and the next, you're fuming over a comment on social media. It's not just you; it's a widespread phenomenon. Let's break down how digital media consumption stirs the pot of our anger and why it feels like our emotions are often just a click away from boiling over.

The Algorithmic Amplification of Anger

Digital platforms, especially social media, are engineered to capture and hold our attention. They use algorithms that prioritize content likely to evoke strong reactions—often anger and outrage—because, let's face it, intense emotions keep us scrolling. This constant exposure to provocative content can set our default emotional state to 'irritated.'

The Echo Chambers Effect

Online spaces often turn into echo chambers where we're surrounded by voices that echo our own thoughts and beliefs. While this can be comforting, it also means we're less exposed to differing viewpoints, making us more susceptible to feeling angry or defensive when confronted with opposing opinions. It's like we're constantly in a room where everyone's agreeing on how right we are—until someone doesn't. Since you are not accustomed to seeing someone with opposing views, you deem it a threat to your beliefs and go full-on defense mode. And that's the beginning of your digital fury road.

Dehumanization and Anonymity

Digital interactions lack the nuances of face-to-face communication— there's no body language, tone of voice, or immediate feedback. This can lead to dehumanization, where we forget there's a real person behind the screen. Plus, the anonymity of the internet can embolden people to say things they'd never say in person, often fueling conflicts and anger.

Constant Connectivity and Overload

Being always connected means we're constantly bombarded with information, much of it negative. News about global disasters, political strife, or even local issues can overwhelm us, contributing to a state of perpetual anger or anxiety. It's like our emotional systems are constantly being overloaded, leaving us no time to process or recover. During the COVID-19 pandemic, a study published in the International Journal of Public Health identified communication overload as a predictor of depressive symptoms. This suggests that increased social media usage correlates with heightened negative emotions, potentially leading to overwhelming feelings.

Breaking the Cycle

Understanding the impact of digital media on our emotions is the first step towards managing our digital diet in a way that serves us, rather than stirs us up. It's about becoming mindful of how our online habits shape our emotions and taking active steps to counteract the negative influences.

The digital age has transformed how we experience and express anger. By recognizing the patterns of our responses to digital media consumption, we can influence our emotions and start to take control back, choosing how we engage with the digital world to support our emotional well-being.

Healthy Digital Habits to Reduce Frustration

- Setting boundaries on screen time
- Cultivating mindfulness
- prioritizing meaningful connections

In the vast expanse of the digital world, it's easy to fall into patterns that crank up our stress levels without even realizing it. But, with a few tweaks and mindful practices, we can navigate the online space in a way that keeps our peace intact. Let's dive into some healthy digital habits that can help dial down the frustration and make our digital interactions more positive.

Curate Your Feed for Positivity

Audit Your Social Media: Take a hard look at your social media feeds. Do certain accounts or pages spark joy, or do they leave you feeling drained or annoyed? It's time to be ruthless with that unfollow button. Prioritize content that uplifts you, educates you, or makes you genuinely happy.

Follow Diverse Voices: While staying within our echo chambers is comfortable, intentionally following accounts with different perspectives can broaden our understanding and reduce frustration born out of misunderstanding or fear of the 'other.'

Set Boundaries and Limits

Screen Time Limits: Most devices now offer tools to monitor and limit screen time. Setting daily limits for specific apps or overall screen time can prevent the endless scroll phenomenon, giving your brain a much-needed break.

Designated Tech-Free Times: Establish tech-free zones or times, such as during meals or an hour before bed, to disconnect and engage with the world around you. This can improve your mood and sleep quality, reducing irritation.

Engage Mindfully

Think Before You Click: Before diving into the comments section or sharing content, take a moment to consider its impact. Is it contributing positively? Could it be misinterpreted? Sometimes, the best action is no action.

Pause Before Responding: When something online does upset you, give yourself a cooling-off period before responding. This pause can be the difference between a heated exchange and a constructive conversation.

Embrace Digital Tools for Wellbeing

Use Apps to Your Advantage: There are countless apps designed to promote relaxation, mindfulness, and positive habits. Whether it's meditation apps like Headspace or Calm, habit trackers, or mood diaries, technology can be a powerful ally in managing your mental health.

Regular Digital Detoxes

Schedule Digital Detox Days: Periodically, take a full day or even a weekend away from digital devices. Use this time to reconnect with offline activities you enjoy, whether it's spending time in nature, reading, or engaging in hobbies that don't involve a screen.

Be Intentional with Your Digital Consumption: Instead of mindlessly consuming whatever comes your way, be selective about the content you engage with. Choose quality over quantity, and prefer content that adds value to your life.

Reflect on Your Digital Habits

Journal About Your Experiences: Keep a log of how certain digital habits affect your mood and stress levels. Reflecting on this can help you identify patterns and make more informed choices about your digital consumption.

Developing healthy digital habits isn't about demonizing technology but about fostering a relationship with our digital devices and platforms that serves us, not drains us. By implementing these strategies, we can enjoy the benefits of the digital age without letting it hijack our emotions.

Did You Know?

We often feel angry simply because we are hungry. Hunger triggering anger is linked to blood sugar drops and stress hormone releases, primed by evolutionary responses to prioritize food-seeking. This can impair emotional regulation and amplify irritability, affecting mood and behavior.

Technology for Anger Management

In an age where technology often gets a bad rap for exacerbating our stress and anger, it's refreshing to flip the script and explore how the very same technology can be a powerful ally in managing those emotions. Let's see how we can harness technology to keep our temper in check and maintain our cool.

Apps and Online Platforms for Anger Management

Mindfulness and Meditation Apps: Tools like Headspace, Calm, and Insight Timer offer guided meditations specifically designed to help with anger management. These apps can teach you mindfulness techniques to stay present and reduce the intensity of your emotions.

Mood Tracking Apps: Apps like Daylio, Moodpath, or Sanvello allow you to track your moods and activities, helping you identify triggers that lead to anger. By understanding patterns in your emotional responses, you can better manage situations that might set you off.

Cognitive Behavioral Therapy (CBT) Apps: Platforms like MoodKit and Woebot use CBT principles to help you challenge and change negative thought patterns that contribute to anger. They offer practical exercises and coping strategies that you can apply in everyday situations.

> Technology serves as a valuable ally in managing anger, providing innovative solutions for emotional regulation and self-awareness.

Virtual Reality (VR) for Emotional Regulation: Emerging VR technology is being used to create immersive environments where individuals can practice relaxation techniques, encounter triggers in a controlled setting, and learn to manage their responses. This hands-on approach offers a safe space to practice new skills without real-world consequences.

Online Learning Resources

Anger Management Courses: Websites like Coursera, Udemy, and Khan Academy offer courses and workshops on anger management, emotional intelligence, and communication skills. These platforms provide access to expert knowledge that can help you understand and manage your anger more effectively.

Podcasts and YouTube Channels: A wealth of free content is available to educate on emotional well-being and anger management. Listening to experts and others' experiences can offer new perspectives and coping strategies. However, beware of fake gurus or people who extort money while overpromising a life of serenity.

Leveraging Social Media Positively

Follow Mental Health Advocates: Social media, when curated mindfully, can be a source of support and inspiration. Following psychologists, therapists, and mental health advocates can provide daily tips and reminders for managing anger and stress.

Join Supportive Communities: Online forums and social media groups can offer a sense of community and understanding. Sharing experiences and coping strategies with others who are working through similar issues can be incredibly validating and helpful.

Digital Detox for Emotional Balance

Digital Detox Apps: Ironically, there are apps designed to help you spend less time on your phone or online. Tools like Forest, Freedom, and Offtime help you limit your screen time, so you can take breaks from the digital world, reducing stress and potential triggers of anger.

Harnessing technology for anger management is about being intentional with how we use digital tools. By selecting apps and resources that support our emotional well-being, we can transform our relationship with technology into one that empowers us to live more balanced and peaceful lives.

Digital Detox Plans

In a world where our lives are increasingly intertwined with digital devices, the idea of a digital detox has become more appealing and necessary. Disconnecting from digital stimuli can significantly reduce tech-induced stress and anger, offering a much-needed respite for our brains. Here's how to embark on a digital detox journey, with plans and challenges designed to reset your digital habits and restore emotional balance.

Starter Digital Detox Plan

Duration: One weekend (Saturday and Sunday)
Rules:
No Social Media: Log out from all social media accounts. If necessary, delete the apps temporarily to avoid temptation.

Limit Screen Time: Use your device only for essential tasks such as calls, texts, and necessary apps (e.g., navigation or music).

No Digital Entertainment: Swap digital forms of entertainment with offline activities. Read a book, go for a hike, or try a new hobby.

Mindful Technology Use: For the technology you do use, be fully present and intentional. Listen to a music album from start to finish, or call a friend for a meaningful conversation.

Challenge: Spend at least 3 hours in nature over the weekend without any digital devices.

Intermediate Digital Detox Plan

Duration: One week
Preparation:
Notify Close Contacts: Let friends, family, and work colleagues know about your detox plan. This will reduce anxiety about missing out or being unreachable.
Set an Autoresponder: If applicable, set up an email autoresponder indicating you're on a digital detox and when you'll be back online.
Rules:
Establish Tech-Free Zones: Make your bedroom and dining area tech-free zones. Charge devices in a different room.
Scheduled Check-ins: Designate two 30-minute slots per day for checking emails and messages.
Evening Wind-down: No screens at least one hour before bedtime to improve sleep quality.
Engage in Physical Activity: Replace some of your usual screen time with physical activity. Aim for at least 30 minutes of exercise each day.
Challenge: Complete a project or activity you've been putting off due to lack of time.

Advanced Digital Detox Challenge

Duration: One month
Preparation:
Digital Clutter Cleanse: Unsubscribe from unnecessary emails, unfollow accounts that don't add value, and delete unused apps.
Set Clear Objectives: Identify what you want to achieve during this detox. More time with family? Start a new project? Read more books?
Rules:

Strict Screen Time Limits: Use digital wellbeing tools to set strict daily limits for your usage.

Replace Digital Habits: Identify the times you're most likely to mindlessly scroll or consume digital content and plan alternative activities.

Key Takeaways

- Digital media, while a significant part of modern life, can exacerbate stress and anger through constant connectivity and exposure to negative content.
- Developing healthy digital habits, such as curating positive content, setting screen time limits, and engaging in digital detoxes, can mitigate these effects.
- Technology also offers tools for managing anger, from mindfulness apps to online resources, turning potential sources of stress into allies for emotional well-being.
- Regular digital detoxes provide a valuable reset for our relationship with technology, reducing tech-induced stress and fostering real-world connections and activities.

Summary of Actionable Steps

- **Curate Your Digital Environment**: Regularly review and adjust your social media feeds to ensure they contribute positively to your day.
- **Implement Screen Time Limits:** Use built-in digital wellbeing tools to set and adhere to daily screen time limits.
- **Engage in Regular Digital Detoxes:** Schedule periodic digital detoxes, ranging from a few hours to a full weekend, to disconnect and recharge.
- **Leverage Apps for Mental Health:** Explore and utilize apps designed for mindfulness, mood tracking, and stress management.
- **Mindful Consumption:** Be deliberate about when and why you engage with digital media, choosing quality over quantity.

The next chapter covers the complex world of interpersonal connections. Discover how to apply emotional intelligence to foster understanding, empathy, and resilience in your relationships. From decoding emotional cues to managing conflicts constructively, we're setting the stage for healthier, more fulfilling interactions.

CHAPTER 9

Seeking Support and Professional Help

The greatest discovery of any generation is that a human being can alter his life by altering his attitude.
— William James

WHAT IF THE key to managing your anger didn't lie in suppressing it but in understanding and channeling it with professional guidance? In a world where mental health is gaining much-needed attention, seeking support and professional help for anger management is not just a sign of strength but a step towards profound personal growth.

> Seeking professional help for anger management is not only a sign of strength but also a pivotal step toward personal growth and emotional well-being.

This chapter is a guide through the landscape of professional help for anger management. From knowing when it's time to seek help, to the transformative role of therapy, the support of peers, and a toolkit of resources and contacts, we're navigating the path to a calmer, more centered you.

When to Seek Help for Anger Issues

Recognizing when to seek help for anger issues is crucial for better emotional health and relationships. Anger, in itself, is a normal, healthy emotion. However, when it spirals out of control, becomes destructive, or negatively impacts your life and the lives of those around you, it's time to consider professional help. Here are some clear signs that indicate it might be time to reach out for support:

1. Frequent Outbursts

If you find yourself frequently losing your temper over minor inconveniences or daily irritations, it's a sign that your anger is not under control. Frequent outbursts can strain relationships and create a cycle of regret and frustration.

2. Physical Symptoms

When you're really mad or frustrated about something, it's not just something you feel inside your head. This anger can actually show up in your body in different ways. For example, you might start getting headaches often, or your stomach might hurt. Some people find it hard to sleep, or they might feel more worried and anxious than usual.

Let's say every time you have to work on a big project with a team, you start feeling super stressed and angry because you end up doing most of the work. You might notice that during these times, you also start having trouble sleeping, you're getting headaches a lot, or your stomach is upset. These physical problems are your body's way of telling you something is wrong.

In this case, the physical symptoms are tied to your feelings of anger and frustration about the unfair workload. Your body is reacting to these emotions. To feel better, it's important to deal with the reason you're feeling so angry in the first place. Talking to your team about sharing the work more fairly could help ease both your anger and the physical symptoms that come with it.

3. Impact on Relationships

When anger leads to frequent arguments, resentment, or even fear among family, friends, or coworkers, it's a significant indicator that professional guidance could help. Healthy relationships should not be consistently jeopardized by unmanaged anger.

4. Regretful Actions

If you often find yourself regretting things said or done in anger, or if your reactions surprise or scare you, these are strong signals that your anger is controlling you, rather than the other way around.

5. Dependence on Substances

Turning to alcohol, drugs, or other substances to "cool off" or manage your mood after an angry outburst is a red flag. This can indicate an unhealthy coping mechanism for dealing with emotional stress.

6. Feedback from Others

Sometimes, it's those around us who notice our need for help first. If people you trust suggest you might benefit from anger management or therapy, consider their perspective seriously.

7. Legal or Occupational Problems

Facing legal issues, such as being ordered by a court to attend anger management classes, or experiencing disciplinary actions at work due to anger, are clear indications that professional help is needed.

8. Feeling Out of Control

A sense of helplessness or feeling out of control when angry, as if you're watching yourself from the outside, suggests that your anger is more intense than what's typically manageable on your own.

9. Desire for Change

Ultimately, recognizing that you want to change your relationship with anger and not knowing how to start is a sufficient reason to seek professional help.

10. Taking the Step

Acknowledging that you might need help managing your anger is a brave and significant first step towards healing. Professional therapists or counselors can provide the tools and strategies to effectively understand and manage your anger, leading to a healthier, more balanced life. Remember, seeking help is a sign of strength, not weakness.

Did You Know?

Anger is a secondary emotion. It is always succeeded by another emotional state. It may be triggered by guilt, stress, trauma or any other underlying mental health issues. This is why professional therapy and counseling helps greatly with anger management because it addresses the root of the problem.

The Role of Counseling and Therapy

The role of therapy isn't just about quelling the flames of anger but understanding its origins, discovering healthier ways to express emotions, and fundamentally changing how we interact with ourselves and others. Let's explore the myriad benefits of therapy and counseling in managing anger:

Understanding the Roots of Anger

Therapy provides a safe and confidential environment where you can delve into the underlying causes of your anger. Whether it stems from past trauma, unresolved conflicts, stress, or anxiety, understanding the root cause is the first step toward effective management.

> Unraveling the underlying causes of anger can pave the way for effective management and emotional healing.

Imagine you've always been quick to anger, and you're not really sure why. Simple things set you off, like someone cutting in line or a friend being late. So, you decide to talk to a therapist because you want to understand what's going on and how to handle it better.

In therapy, you have a quiet, private space to really dig into your feelings. You start talking about your life and soon realize that your anger might be coming from something that happened when you were younger. Maybe you felt ignored or like you had to be perfect all the time to get any attention. Or perhaps there was a time you felt very let down or scared, and you never really talked about it or dealt with it.

By discussing these past experiences, you start to see how they've been like invisible strings, pulling at your emotions and making you react with anger in situations that remind you, even a little, of those old feelings of being ignored or scared.

Understanding this connection doesn't fix everything right away, but it's like turning on a light in a dark room. Suddenly, you see why you've been bumping into things. With the therapist's help, you start learning new ways to deal with situations that used to make you mad. You learn how to pause, think about why you're really upset, and respond in a way that feels better for you and those around you.

Learning Healthy Expression

When you're dealing with anger, it's crucial to find ways to let it out without hurting yourself or the people around you. That's where counseling comes in handy. It's like a class where you learn the best ways to deal with your feelings.

One major lesson is about being assertive. This means you learn how to say what's on your mind and stand up for yourself, but in a way that's respectful to others. It's about being clear and direct without being mean or aggressive.

Another thing you'll work on is figuring out how to solve problems without making the situation worse. This can mean learning how to talk things through and find solutions that work for everyone, instead of letting a disagreement turn into a big fight.

Discovering healthy ways to express yourself can lead to more meaningful interactions and greater emotional well-being.

You'll also pick up tips on how to keep your cool. This includes strategies like taking deep breaths when you're upset, stepping away from a situation until you feel calmer, and thinking things through before you react.

Learning these skills helps keep your anger from getting out of hand and leading to actions you might regret later. Plus, it's not just about avoiding bad outcomes; it's about building better, stronger relationships with the people in your life and feeling more in control and at peace with yourself.

Improving Self-awareness

Through therapy, individuals gain increased self-awareness about their emotional triggers and the physical and emotional signs that anger is building. This awareness allows for the early implementation of coping strategies before emotions become overwhelming.

You notice that every time someone interrupts you while you're talking, you get really upset. In therapy, you start paying attention to how this makes your heart race and your hands clench. You realize these are your body's way of telling you you're getting angry. Now that you know this, as soon as someone cuts you off and you feel that rush, you remember to take a deep breath and count to ten before you respond. This way, you're catching your anger early and dealing with it calmly, instead of letting it explode.

Reducing Physical and Emotional Impact

Chronic anger can have significant physical and emotional consequences, including increased risk of heart disease, depression, and anxiety. Therapy can reduce these risks by helping individuals manage their anger more effectively, leading to a healthier and more balanced life.

Let's say you used to get angry a lot, and you noticed it was making you feel tired all the time, and you were often sad or worried. After a while in therapy, you learn how to handle things that used to make you mad by talking about your feelings or going for a walk to cool off. As you get better at managing your anger, you start feeling more energetic and happier. Your worries don't weigh as heavy on you anymore. This shows how getting a grip on your anger not only makes you feel better mentally but can also improve your overall health.

Enhancing Relationships

Anger can strain relationships, causing damage that might seem irreparable. Counseling offers strategies for repairing and strengthening relationships through improved communication, empathy, and understanding. It teaches how to handle disagreements in a healthy manner, fostering closer and more fulfilling relationships.

Picture this: You and your best friend have a big argument over something small, like who forgot to pay for lunch last time. It turns into a shouting match, leaving both of you upset and not talking. In counseling, you learn how to talk things out without getting mad. Next time a disagreement comes up, you remember to listen first and try to see things from your friend's point of view. You calmly explain how you feel and understand where they're coming from too. By doing this, you both feel heard and understood. Not only is the issue resolved without hurting feelings, but your friendship also gets stronger because you've shown each other respect and empathy.

Preventing Escalation

One of the key benefits of therapy is learning how to prevent anger from escalating. This includes recognizing early signs of frustration and implementing techniques to cool down, such as time-outs, deep breathing, or engaging in physical activity.

Imagine you're in a situation that usually makes you blow your top, like being stuck in traffic when you're already late. You start feeling that familiar annoyance bubble up. But then you remember what you learned in therapy about catching your anger before it blows. You take a deep breath, turn on some music, and remind yourself that getting angry won't clear the traffic. You might even pull over to stretch your legs or do some quick exercises by the car. These actions help you cool down and keep the situation from getting the best of you. Instead of arriving at your destination fuming and stressed, you manage to stay calm and collected.

Personal Growth

Therapy for anger management is not just about controlling temper. It's a pathway to personal growth, offering insights into emotional patterns and how they affect our lives. This journey can lead to significant improvements in overall well-being and life satisfaction.

Think of therapy not just as a way to keep your temper in check but as a journey that helps you grow as a person. It's like getting a map that shows you how your feelings shape your actions and impact your life. This journey can make you happier and more satisfied with life because you understand yourself better and know how to handle your emotions.

Tailored Strategies

Counseling provides personalized strategies that are tailored to an individual's specific needs and life circumstances. What works for one person might not work for another, and therapists can help identify the most effective methods for each individual.

When you go to counseling, you get advice that fits just right for you. It's like having a custom-made plan for handling anger, because what helps one person stay calm might not work for someone else. Your therapist works with you to figure out the best ways for you to deal with tricky situations, based on what you're going through in life.

Support and Accountability

Therapists provide a supportive environment that encourages progress while holding individuals accountable for their actions and growth. This combination of support and accountability is crucial for making long-lasting changes.

Your therapist is like a coach cheering you on, but also like a trainer who makes sure you're sticking to your goals. They're there to celebrate your wins and help you learn from the tough times, making sure you're always moving forward. This mix of cheering and gentle nudging is what helps you make real, lasting changes.

Empowerment

Ultimately, therapy empowers individuals to take control of their anger and their lives. It provides the tools and confidence needed to face challenges in a healthier, more constructive way.

Engaging in therapy or counseling for anger management is an investment in your emotional and physical health, relationships, and future. It's about building a life where anger no longer controls your actions or dictates the quality of your interactions with the world.

At the end of the day, therapy gives you the power over your anger and your life. It's like being handed the steering wheel and the roadmap, so you can drive through challenges without getting lost in anger. With the right tools and confidence, you're ready to face whatever comes your way in a calm and positive manner.

Going to therapy for anger management is more than just learning to cool down—it's about investing in a happier, healthier you. It's building a life where anger doesn't get to make the rules, letting you enjoy better health, stronger relationships, and a brighter future.

Support Groups and Peer Assistance

Support groups and peer assistance play a crucial role in the journey toward managing anger effectively. These platforms offer a unique form of support that complements individual therapy, providing a community where experiences, struggles, and successes are shared openly. Let's dive into why support groups and peer assistance are so valuable for those dealing with anger issues.

Support groups and peer assistance offer invaluable companionship and understanding on the path to managing anger, providing a safe space for sharing experiences and receiving communal support.

Shared Experiences

One of the most powerful aspects of support groups is the realization that you're not alone in your struggle. Hearing others share similar feelings, challenges, and triumphs can be incredibly validating and comforting. This shared experience fosters a sense of belonging and community.

127

Diverse Perspectives

In a support group, members come from various backgrounds and have different life stories, yet they share a common goal. This diversity offers a wealth of perspectives and strategies for managing anger, providing members with a broader toolkit of coping mechanisms.

Safe and Non-judgmental Space

Support groups provide a safe, confidential, and non-judgmental environment where individuals can express their feelings and experiences without fear of criticism. This openness encourages honesty and vulnerability, which are key to personal growth and understanding.

Learning Through Others

Witnessing how others navigate their anger issues can be an educational and enlightening experience. Members can learn from each other's successes and setbacks, gaining insights into what might or might not work for them in their own journey.

Peer Encouragement and Motivation

The encouragement and motivation from peers who understand the challenges of managing anger can be a powerful motivator. Celebrating each other's progress, no matter how small, can boost morale and encourage persistence, especially during tough times.

Accountability

Being part of a group provides a level of accountability that can be motivating. Knowing that others are aware of your goals and progress can push you to stay committed to your anger management journey.

Cost-effective Support

While individual therapy can be an essential part of managing anger, it can also be costly. Support groups often offer a more affordable way to receive support, making them accessible to a wider range of people.

Building Coping Skills

Through discussions and sharing, members of support groups can learn effective coping skills and strategies for dealing with triggers and stressful situations. This practical advice is grounded in real-life experiences, making it highly relevant and applicable.

Enhancing Emotional Intelligence

Participating in support groups can improve emotional intelligence by increasing empathy, enhancing communication skills, and fostering better relationships. Learning to understand and respond to others' emotions can, in turn, offer deeper insights into one's own emotional patterns.

Continuous Support

Finally, support groups provide an ongoing source of support. Unlike therapy, which may have a set number of sessions, support groups can offer long-term companionship on the journey toward managing anger, adapting and growing with its members over time.

In essence, support groups and peer assistance embody the principle that together, we are stronger. They offer a space not just for managing anger but for transforming it into a force for positive change, both within oneself and within the community.

Resources and Contact Information

Finding the right resources and contacts for professional help with anger management can be the first step towards a healthier way of managing emotions. Below is a compilation of various resources, including websites, hotlines, and organizations that specialize in anger management and mental health support. This list aims to provide a starting point for those seeking assistance.

Websites for Information and Support

- **American Psychological Association (APA): apa.org**

Offers a wealth of information on anger management, including articles, tips, and research findings.

- **National Institute of Mental Health (NIMH): nimh.nih.gov**

Provides detailed information on anger and other mental health issues, including symptoms, treatments, and current research.

- **Mind (UK): mind.org.uk**

Offers support and advice on anger management, mental health problems, and where to find help in the UK.

- **Mental Health America (MHA): mhanational.org**

Contains resources on understanding anger, self-help tools, and how to get help.

Therapy and Counseling Services

BetterHelp: betterhelp.com

An online platform providing access to licensed therapists for help with anger management and other mental health issues.

    o **Talkspace: talkspace.com**

Offers online therapy with professionals that can assist with anger management techniques and strategies.

Hotlines for Immediate Support

    o **National Suicide Prevention Lifeline (USA):** 1-800-273-TALK (1-800-273-8255)

Available 24/7 for anyone in distress. While not specific to anger management, they can provide immediate support and resources.

    o **Crisis Text Line (USA):** Text HOME to 741741

A text-based support service available 24/7 for any crisis, including those struggling with anger.

Support Groups

    o **Anger Management Groups**: Check local community centers, hospitals, or mental health clinics for anger management group sessions near you.

    o **Mental Health America (MHA) Support Community**: mhanational.org

Provides a directory to help find support groups for a variety of mental health issues, including anger management.

Additional Resources

o **SAMHSA's National Helpline (USA):** 1-800-662-HELP (1-800-662-4357)

Offers general information on mental health and can help locate treatment services and support groups.

o **Relate (UK): relate.org.uk**

Provides relationship support, including help with managing anger within relationships.

This list is not exhaustive, but it provides a solid foundation for seeking help. Remember, reaching out for support is a sign of strength and the first step towards taking control of your anger and improving your quality of life.

Key Takeaways

- Understanding the signs that indicate when professional help is needed for anger management is crucial.
- These interventions provide valuable insights into the causes of anger, teach healthy expression, and promote personal growth.
- Sharing experiences and strategies within a supportive community can be incredibly validating and helpful.
- A variety of resources, including websites, hotlines, and organizations, are available to provide support and guidance on managing anger effectively.

Summary of Actionable Steps

- Pay attention to frequent outbursts, impacts on relationships, and feelings of regret as indicators that it's time to seek help.

- Consider counseling or therapy to uncover the roots of your anger and learn healthy coping mechanisms.
- Connect with others facing similar challenges to share experiences and learn from each other.
- Make use of the resources and contacts listed to find professional help tailored to your needs.
- Remember, seeking help and working on managing your anger is a sign of strength and a step towards personal growth.

As we turn the page from seeking support and professional help, we're equipped with the knowledge and tools to take the next steps on our journey toward emotional well-being.

In the next chapter, "Building a Resilient Mindset," we'll dive into strategies for cultivating resilience. Discover how resilience can not only help you bounce back from setbacks but also transform how you approach challenges, leading to a more fulfilling and balanced life.

CHAPTER 10

Moving Forward with Confidence

> *It is not the strongest of the species that survive, nor the most intelligent, but the one most responsive to change.*
>
> **– Charles Darwin**

IMAGINE STANDING AT the edge of a vast ocean, the waves of anger and frustration that once threatened to pull you under now ripple calmly at your feet. You've learned to navigate these waters with skill, but the journey doesn't end here. This chapter is about sailing forward with confidence, using the tools and insights you've gathered to maintain your course toward emotional well-being.

In Chapter 10 equipped with strategies to confront future challenges and embrace emotional well-being with confidence.

In Chapter 10, we'll explore strategies for maintaining progress in anger management, preparing for future challenges, and embracing a future of emotional well-being. With each step, you'll learn how to build on your achievements and face the future positively and confidently.

Maintaining Progress in Anger Management

Maintaining progress in anger management is a journey, not a destination. It involves ongoing effort and commitment to applying the strategies you've learned and adapting them as your life changes. Here are some valuable pieces of advice to help you continue building upon the progress you've made in managing your anger effectively:

Establish a Routine for Sef-reflection

Regular Reflection: Set aside time each week to reflect on your emotional responses and situations that provoked anger. Assess what strategies worked and where there's room for improvement.

Reflect on Setbacks: View any setbacks not as failures but as opportunities for learning and growth. Analyze what happened and how you can adjust your response in the future.

Continue Learning and Growth

Educational Resources: Stay engaged with books, podcasts, and articles about anger management and emotional intelligence. Continuous learning can provide new insights and reinforce existing strategies.

Workshops and Seminars: Participate in workshops or seminars focused on anger management, communication skills, and stress relief. These can offer fresh perspectives and tools for handling emotions.

Keep nurturing your growth and knowledge. There's always more to learn and explore on your journey toward better anger management.

Implement Healthy Lifestyle Choices

Physical Activity: Regular exercise is a powerful tool for managing stress and anger. Find physical activities you enjoy and make them a part of your routine.

Balanced Diet: Nutrition can affect your mood and emotional responses. Aim for a balanced diet that supports overall well-being.

Focus on Positive Relationships

Nurture Positive Relationships: Invest time and energy in relationships that support your growth and well-being. Positive interactions can serve as a buffer against stress and anger.

Communication Skills: Continue to hone your communication skills, practicing assertiveness and active listening. Effective communication can prevent misunderstandings that might lead to anger.

Maintaining progress in anger management is an active process that evolves over time. By incorporating these strategies into your life, you reinforce your foundation and set the stage for continued growth and emotional resilience.

Some practical examples!

Carlos grew up in a home where anger was the default emotion. He found himself repeating this pattern with his own family, which broke his heart. He knew he had to break the cycle but wasn't sure how.

Carlos sought help through counseling, where he learned about the concept of "generational anger." He worked on understanding his family's history with anger and developed strategies for expressing his emotions in healthier ways. He also started family meetings where everyone could share their feelings in a safe space.

This new approach brought Carlos's family closer. They learned to express their frustrations without anger, strengthening their bond. Carlos felt proud to be changing his family's emotional legacy, showing that it's possible to break free from harmful patterns and build something healthier for the next generation.

Preparing for Future Challenges

Navigating future anger-inducing situations with grace and resilience is crucial for maintaining your progress in anger management. Life is unpredictable, but being equipped with the right tools can help you face challenges without reverting to old patterns. Here's how to prepare yourself for whatever lies ahead:

> Equip yourself with the right tools and mindset to navigate future challenges with grace and resilience, ensuring continued progress in managing anger effectively.

Anticipate and Plan

Develop a Response Plan: For each potential trigger, develop a strategy. This might include taking deep breaths, counting to ten, or using positive self-talk to calm down before responding.

Strengthen Your Emotional Toolbox

Expand Coping Strategies: Continue to learn and practice a variety of coping strategies. Techniques such as guided imagery, progressive muscle relaxation, or mindfulness meditation can be powerful tools in different situations.

Practice Scenario-based Responses: Mentally rehearse how you would like to respond in challenging scenarios. Visualization can help prepare you to act in accordance with your values and goals when faced with real-life triggers.

Maintain Emotional Balance

Regular Self-care: Engage in activities that promote well-being and relaxation on a regular basis. Whether it's exercise, reading, or spending time in nature, self-care practices can reduce overall stress levels and make you less susceptible to anger.

Foster Supportive Relationships

Communicate Your Goals: Share your anger management goals with close friends or family. They can offer support, understanding, and sometimes a helpful perspective during difficult times.

Learn from Experiences

View Challenges as Opportunities: Approach each challenging situation as an opportunity to practice your skills and learn. Reflect on what worked and what didn't, and adjust your strategies accordingly.

Celebrate Successes: Recognize and celebrate when you successfully manage a difficult situation. Acknowledging your progress reinforces positive behavior and boosts your confidence.

Stay Flexible and Adaptable

Be Open to Change: Understand that what works for you now might need to be adjusted in the future. Stay open to exploring new strategies and adapting your approach as you grow and change.

> Stay flexible and adaptable, for the path to managing anger effectively often requires adjustments along the way.

By preparing yourself with these tools and strategies, you're not just ready to face future challenges; you're setting yourself up to continue your journey of emotional growth and resilience with confidence.

Key Takeaways

- Maintaining progress in anger management requires consistent practice of the strategies learned.
- Preparing for future challenges involves anticipating potential triggers and planning healthy responses.

- Fostering a positive outlook is essential for emotional well-being, including practicing gratitude and surrounding yourself with positive influences.
- Resilience is strengthened by embracing challenges, developing a growth mindset, and nurturing emotional intelligence.
- Open communication and a strong support network are vital for emotional health.
- Continuous learning and being open to feedback contribute to personal growth.
- Regular mindfulness practice and self-care rituals are crucial for maintaining mental, physical, and emotional balance.

Summary of Actionable Steps

- Write down three things you're grateful for each day to cultivate positivity.
- Set a goal to learn something new about managing emotions or personal development every month.
- Dedicate time each week to connect with friends, family, or support groups.

Like Dana's temper was affecting her friendships. She'd snap at minor annoyances, regretting it later. She wanted to find a way to deal with her anger without losing friends.

Dana discovered that painting allowed her to express her feelings without words. She set up a small studio in her home and whenever she felt the anger rising, she'd turn to her canvas instead of lashing out.

Painting became Dana's way of processing her emotions. Her friends noticed the positive change in her behavior, and Dana felt more at peace with herself. Her story illustrates the power of creative expression in managing emotions and healing relationships.

With the tools and strategies outlined in this chapter, you're now equipped to move forward with confidence, building upon your progress and facing future challenges with resilience and positivity.

CONCLUSION

ONGRATULATIONS ON COMPLETING your learning journey about managing your anger issues. It takes tremendous courage to choose a path of self-improvement because, at its threshold, you must leave your ego and embrace your flaws. An Austrian poet, Rainer Maria Rilke once said, "The only journey is the journey within." And the fact that you are here on this page testifies that you have already taken the most vital steps toward enhancing the quality of your life, inside out.

This book has probed into the nuanced world of teenage anger, providing insights, strategies, and tools to navigate this under-discussed and confusing aspect of a teenager's life. As we conclude our exploration, let's take a moment to reflect on the most important lessons learned and vow to move forward with confidence.

Throughout this guide, we have discussed the multifaceted nature of anger in teenage life, dissecting its triggers, physiological responses, and emotional implications. We've debunked common misconceptions and equipped ourselves with a deeper understanding of the teenage brain's role in anger dynamics.

We've learned to recognize and understand our anger, identifying personal triggers and mastering the art of emotional self-awareness. By exploring anger's physical and emotional dimensions, we've gained invaluable insights into managing and de-escalating anger before it spirals out of control.

We have learned to improve our relationships and shield our loved ones from unreasonable outbursts of anger by learning the importance of healthy boundary-setting and effective communication strategies.

Building upon this foundation, we've honed our emotional intelligence, developing the skills of managing expectations, frustrations, and cultivating self-control in various scenarios.

Our journey has also led us to explore coping mechanisms and techniques, from mindfulness practices to assertive communication skills, offering practical tools for immediate relief and long-term anger management.

Examining the impact of technology on anger and embracing healthy digital habits, we have explored what it is like to harness technology positively for managing anger.

As you conclude this book and transition to its practical applications, remember that you are not alone. As discussed within the book, acknowledge the significance of seeking support and professional assistance. Embrace the benefits of counseling and therapy, as well as the value of support groups and peer assistance.

It's time to move forward with confidence. Let us remember to maintain progress in anger management and prepare ourselves for future challenges with resilience and a positive outlook.

Now armed with a wealth of knowledge and practical strategies, I encourage you to go forth and apply these tools in your daily life. Embrace the journey of self-discovery and personal growth, knowing that each step you take brings you closer to emotional well-being and healthier relationships.

Spreading the Wisdom
Empower Others with Your Insight

Now that you've acquired all the tools to master your emotions and navigate the challenges of anger, it's time to pay it forward and guide other readers toward the same enlightenment.

Simply by sharing your genuine thoughts about this book on Amazon, you'll not only help fellow teenagers find the guidance they seek but also ignite their passion for understanding and managing their anger.

Thank you for your invaluable contribution. The journey toward mastering anger is sustained when we pass on our knowledge—and you're playing a crucial role in that endeavor.

Leave a review

ABOUT THE AUTHOR

EMMA DAVIS is a woman who wears many hats. She is a clinical social worker, a therapist, and a financial advisor, as well as the author of Effective Anger Management for Teens.

Her books are aimed at teenagers, covering a diverse range of topics, including life and coping skills, DBT techniques, finances, puberty, developing a growth mindset, and career planning. She focuses on the unique challenges faced by adolescents in their emotional and physiological development, empowering readers with a strong foundation for understanding.

Emma draws on experience and knowledge from all her roles, as well as her experience as a mother, to guide young people through the difficult stage of adolescence. She runs a therapy practice and financial education agency tailored to teenagers, and has worked with a diverse range of young people facing different practical and emotional challenges. She also runs several online courses on cultivating interpersonal skills, gratitude, happiness, and joy, as well as 10 residential care facilities for adults with disabilities and mental health challenges, which also informs her work.

Emma is married with 9 children between the ages of 3 and 22. She enjoys spending time with her family, practicing jiu jitsu, and developing her skills in photography.

Helping Teens With Finances, Anger Management, Mental Health, And Future Life Planning

From
EMMA DAVIS

Available on Amazon or wherever books are sold

To learn more about helping teens with finances, anger management, mental health, and future life planning

please join my newsletter!

at www.emmadavisbooks.com

REFERENCES

1. Spielberger, C. D., Krasner, S. S., & Solomon, E. P. (1988, January 1). The Experience, Expression, and Control of Anger. Contributions to Psychology and Medicine. https://doi.org/10.1007/978-1-4612-3824-9_5

2. Batrinos, M. L. (2012). Testosterone and aggressive behavior in man. International journal of endocrinology and metabolism, 10(3), 563.

3. Šimić, G., Tkalčić, M., Vukić, V., Mulc, D., Španić, E., Šagud, M., Olucha-Bordonau, F. E., Vukšić, M., & Hof, P. R. (2021, May 31). Understanding Emotions: Origins and Roles of the Amygdala. Biomolecules. https://doi.org/10.3390/biom11060823

4. Roemmich, J. N., & Rogol, A. D. (1999, January 1). Hormonal changes during puberty and their relationship to fat distribution. Wiley Online Library. https://doi.org/10.1002/(SICI)1520-6300(1999)11:2

5. Castillo-Eito, L., Armitage, C. J., Norman, P., Day, M., Doğru, O. C., & Rowe, R. (2020, June 1). How can adolescent aggression be reduced? A multi-level meta-analysis. Clinical Psychology Review. https://doi.org/10.1016/j.cpr.2020.101853

6. Yadav, P. K., Yadav, R. L., & Sapkota, N. K. (2017). Anger; its impact on human body. Innovare Journal of Health Sciences, 4(5), 3-5.

7. Staicu, M. L., & Cuţov, M. (2010). Anger and health risk behaviors. Journal of medicine and life, 3(4), 372.

8. Friedman, H. H. Overcoming Cognitive Distortions: How to Recognize and Challenge the Thinking Traps that Make You Miserable.

9. Fiess, J., Rockstroh, B., Schmidt, R., & Steffen, A. (2015, December 1). Emotion regulation and functional neurological symptoms: Does emotion processing convert into sensorimotor activity? Journal of Psychosomatic Research (Print). https://doi.org/10.1016/j.jpsychores.2015.10.009

10. Herringa, R. J. (2017, August 19). Trauma, PTSD, and the Developing Brain. Current Psychiatry Reports. https://doi.org/10.1007/s11920-017-0825-3

11. Tang, Y. Y., Tang, R., & Posner, M. I. (2016). Mindfulness meditation improves emotion regulation and reduces drug abuse. Drug and alcohol dependence, 163, S13-S18.

12. Kövecses, Z. (2010, December 14). Anger: Its language, conceptualization, and physiology in the light of cross-cultural evidence. De Gruyter. https://www.degruyter.com/document/doi/10.1515/9783110809305.181/pdf?licenseType=restricted

13. von Salisch, M., & Vogelgesang, J. (2005). Anger regulation among friends: Assessment and development from childhood to adolescence. Journal of Social and Personal Relationships, 22(6), 837-855.

14. Debaryshe, B. D., & Fryxell, D. (1998). A developmental perspective on anger: Family and peer contexts. Psychology in the Schools, 35(3), 205-216.

15. Issue - Volume 14, July 2017, issue 3. (n.d.). https://biblioscout.net/journal/pm/14/3#page=30

16. Lehane, O. (2019, March 1). Dealing with Frustration: A Grounded Theory Study of CVE Practitioners. DOAJ (DOAJ: Directory of Open Access Journals). https://doi.org/10.4119/ijcv-3105

17. Wright, S. F., Day, A., & Howells, K. (2009, September 1). Mindfulness and the treatment of anger problems. Aggression and Violent Behavior (Print). https://doi.org/10.1016/j.avb.2009.06.008

18. Bickram, S. (2019). A Quantitative Analysis between Anger and Assertiveness Communication Styles among Online Students (Doctoral dissertation, Keiser University).

19. Malmir, R., & Nedaee, T. (2019). The relationship between anger control and physical activity. Health, 21(4), 284-291.

20. Steffen, S. L., & Fothergill, A. (2009, March 1). 9/11 Volunteerism: A pathway to personal healing and community engagement. ⊠the ⊠Social Science Journal/⊠the ⊠Social Science Journal. https://doi.org/10.1016/j.soscij.2008.12.005

21. Sharma, M. K., Sunil, S., Roopesh, B. N., Galagali, P., Anand, N., Thakur, P. C., Singh, P., Ajith, S., & Murthy, K. D. (2020, January 1). Digital failure: An emerging reason of anger expression among adolescents. Industrial Psychiatry Journal/Industrial Psychiatry Journal. https://doi.org/10.4103/ipj.ipj_81_19

22. Wollebæk, D., Karlsen, R., Steen-Johnsen, K., & Enjolras, B. (2019). Anger, fear, and echo chambers: The emotional basis for online behavior. Social Media+ Society, 5(2), 2056305119829859.

23. Almourad, M. B., Alrobai, A., Skinner, T., Hussain, M., & Ali, R. (2021, November 1). Digital wellbeing tools through users lens. Technology in Society (Print). https://doi.org/10.1016/j.techsoc.2021.101778

24. Sadagheyani, H. E., Tatari, F., Raoufian, H., Salimi, P. S., & Gazerani, A. (2021, May 1). The effect of multimedia-based education on students' anger

management skill. Educación Médica (Ed. Impresa). https://doi.org/10.1016/j.edumed.2020.09.020

25. Kassinove, H., & Sukhodolsky, D. G. (1995). Anger disorders: Basic science and practice issues. Issues in comprehensive pediatric nursing, 18(3), 173-205.

26. Üzar-özçetin, Y. S. (n.d.). Effects of Structured Group Counseling on Anger Management Skills of Nursing Students | Journal of Nursing Education. Journal of Nursing Education. https://journals.healio.com/doi/abs/10.3928/01484834-20170222-10